brother Paul

The Road to Immortality

brother Paul

The Road to Immortality

ISBN/EAN: 9783741178474

Manufactured in Europe, USA, Canada, Australia, Japa

Cover: Foto ©Andreas Hilbeck / pixelio.de

Manufactured and distributed by brebook publishing software
(www.brebook.com)

brother Paul

The Road to Immortality

BY BROTHER PAUL.

"We live in deeds, not years; in thoughts, not breaths;
·In feelings, not in figures on a dial.
We should count time by heart-throbs.   He most lives
Who thinks most—feels the noblest—acts the best.
Life's but a means unto an end—that end,
Beginning, mean and end to all things—God."
                                                                    —*Festus.*

———————

ESOTERIC PUBLISHING COMPANY,
APPLEGATE, CALIFORNIA.
1898.

PREFACE.

The thoughts herein expressed are sent forth with an earnest prayer that they may be acceptable, and beneficial to the dear ones who crave that spiritual bread which alone can satisfy the hunger of the soul. The life of consecration and trust in our heavenly Father has been lived by the author for a number of years. These years have been spent with a company of people, who, apart from the world, were all living the same consecrated life. Therefore he feels in a position to speak from absolute knowledge, and that he does not overstate facts in saying, that all who dedicate their lives to God, and live absolutely up to the requirements of the covenant given to Moses on Sinai, will have all their wants supplied, will never suffer sickness or sorrow, and will eventually overcome the ruler of death and the grave. This statement does not apply to those who believe themselves to be living a life of consecration; but only to those who live that life in deed and in truth. Man cannot accomplish this in his own strength, but, as grand old Isaiah truly says, "Trust ye in the Lord forever; for in the Lord JEHOVAH is everlasting strength." Isaiah XXVI. 4.

The life of chastity, as set forth in the following pages, must be adhered to, as no one can consecrate his life to God, unless he is living a life of absolute holiness and purity. This life of chastity is the same as was lived and taught by our Lord Jesus the Christ, nineteen hundred years ago. It is therefore hoped that all zealous Christian men and women who desire to live the Christ life, will give these methods their earnest and prayerful consideration.

All men desire and look forward to a time when they will enjoy an immortal existence, free from disease, sorrow, and

death. They look for this celestial state to obtain after the
physical has been laid in the grave. This belief is a very serious mistake and does much to retard the progress of the soul.
The truth is, that immortality has never been, neither will it
ever be gained, unless the consciousness of the soul has been
awakened while dwelling in a physical body. It was for this
purpose that God gave man a material body. The gateway of
the grave opens into a realm of unconsciousness or semi-con-
sciousness, not into a realm of spiritual, everlasting consciousness; which is the only consciousness that makes man immortal.

An unceasing consciousness can only be obtained while the
spiritual ego inhabits an earthly tabernacle; and this consciousness must be unfolded through the application of methods
in harmony with spiritual law. These laws cannot be lived up
to or understood until the soul has, through the process of evolution, gained a high degree of unfoldment. When the necessary degree of unfoldment has been gained by the soul, it
reaches upward to the Father to know his mind and will.
This reaching upward of the soul is the silent aspiration, or
prayer, that is always answered. God answers all such prayers in these words, "If ye will obey my voice indeed, and
keep my covenant, then ye shall be a peculiar treasure unto
me above all people; for all the earth is mine." Ex. xix. 5.
Therefore, the reason for the necessity of dedicating the life
to God is, that we may have him for our protector. If man
endeavors to gain immortality through his own efforts he will
find only failure.

The atheist, as well as all other classes who reject God and
worship a creation of their own imagination, cannot hope for
an immortal existence; he can expect nothing more in this
world than an intellectual, semi-conscious existence, and in the
world to come a consciousness measured by the attention paid
to spiritual things while on earth. One thing is certain: The
soul of man does not develop after it leaves the body, unless

it has reached a state of unfoldment that permits it to live independent of material conditions.

The purpose of God in creating man, was to produce a being in his image and likeness; they were to have dominion over all the earth, to command and be obeyed. Adam, the father of the present race, had unfolded the image of the Father, but not the likeness, namely, the power to use the creative word; therefore he was not a perfect representative of the word, or thought of God, which will not be fully ultimated until the likeness is attained. Adam, not having unfolded the nature of the perfect man, could not eat of the fruit of the tree of life, and live. But, as it was necessary for the likeness to be attained, he was permitted to eat of the fruit, in order that through experience man might unfold and gain knowledge and understanding. One short earth life is inadequate to produce such a perfect being; if it were, gods would walk among men. Therefore the necessity of re-incarnation, which permits the spiritual ego, the real man, to return again and again to earth, times without number, until he gains knowledge sufficient to enable him to understand the purpose and will of God.

The human family have become so merged into the material elements, and their senses so benumbed by passion and sin, that they cannot comprehend spiritual things. Their physical organism has become so gross that the interior man is unable to manifest through it. They have lost sight of the powers of spirit, which are latent within. They cannot remember the past because they continually deny it, and they will not obtain a remembrance of it until a soul consciousness has been developed. However, knowledge has been stored up by the soul and can be used by it whenever the requisite conditions are gained and maintained. It is only the lower self that prevents the spirit of man from expressing its true nature: when this has been made the server instead of the ruler, man is no longer a mortal, but an immortal; he has gained the dominion over all earthly things, and is a glorified son of God, a king, with power to rule the earth.

We earnestly hope that our readers will give these truths
their earnest consideration. We hope that they will not become discouraged if failure marks their early efforts. They
should bear in mind that, if they would gain immortality, they
must expect to devote years of patient labor to the accomplishment of their purpose; no one can eradicate the evils of
his nature until it has been entirely reformed, or re-created.
The writer is personally acquainted with those who labored ten
years before they overcame the powers of the serpent. Those
who accomplish this in seven years are fortunate indeed. Remember that, if you enlist in this great fight that is to emanci-
pate you from the evils of flesh and give you the dominion
over the powers of death and the grave, you must be prepared
to overcome all obstacles. Refuse to be discouraged, but press
ever onward, feeling that you have been created a son of God,
therefore are able to conquer all the evil influences, seen and
unseen, that would bar your progress and hold you in slavery
to earthly environment and conditions.

To be free, man must feel, nay, desire with all his heart, that
his sins go before him to judgment. This brings much sorrow
and many trials, but trials are necessary in order that man may
learn that if he would be master he must " tread the wine press
alone." He must walk the narrow way unaided by friend or
companion, depending upon no earthly power, but upon the
God of the universe, to help, sustain, and lead.

May the light of God's presence be ever a guide to all those
who strive after the priceless pearl, immortality. It is the cen-
tral jewel in the kingly crown which all will possess after they
have been nailed to the cross, and are clothed in the spotless
garments of eternal life. May the peace of God rest upon
his children; and may his love abide with them forever.

THE AUTHOR.

CHAPTER I.

Sages of every age have sought the *Elixir Vitæ*. Some claimed to have found it, while others, after years of study and research, have declared that "man was born to die," that eternal youth, or an immortal existence in the physical body, is but a delusion, a chimera, a creation of a disordered brain. Whether these wise ones spoke the truth or were themselves deluded, we will leave the reader to decide. If the thoughts herein expressed prove to be of benefit to one soul seeking the light, the object of the writer shall have been accomplished. The soul's prayer, "Oh Father, let thy mind and will control the thought," shall have been answered. If nothing else be attained, at least the writer will have the consciousness that he has acted in accordance with the will of the Father, and in so doing has lessened the distance between himself and the goal of his desires. If the reader is a seeker after truth, then he has but to "prove all things, and hold fast that which is good."

Jesus, the greatest of all teachers and expounders of divine truth, nearly nineteen hundred years ago gave utterance to these words: "But I tell you of a truth, there be some standing here, which shall not taste of death, till they see the kingdom of God." St. Luke IX. 27. The kingdom Jesus spoke of has not yet come; therefore the natural conclusion is, that there is at least one man alive on earth who has retained the physical body for nineteen hundred years. As God's laws are unchangeable, it must follow that all who obey them will obtain similar results. The divine . laws and methods that will produce such marvelous results, we will endeavor to explain. We assure our readers that all who apply these methods faithfully and earnestly, with a determina-

tion that knows no such thing as failure, may drink from the
fountains of eternal youth, may draw wisdom, knowledge, and
understanding direct from the fountainhead of God's own mind.
The individual who can draw sustenance from the Infinite Life,
will be always able to rejuvenate his body and perpetuate his existence. He alone of all the sons of men has dominion over death
and the grave. Before we speak of the laws whereby an immortal existence is made possible, we will try to make plain the
true understanding of the term "immortality."

When the term "immortal life" is used, we do not wish the
reader to understand that the physical body, as we see it manifest to the external sight, is to be retained throughout the end-
less ages of eternity. Undoubtedly there will come a time,
when, of his own free will and desire, the immortal man, the
acknowledged son of God, will willingly lay aside his earthly
house of clay, in order to pass on to higher spheres of service.
The immortal man lives wholly from the realm of mind, and
when his labors here below are finished the physical body will
be no longer needed. It will then become an incumbrance, im-
peding the free action of the spirit. Such an one will, however,
retain his body until his use as a worker on earth is ultimated,
be it one hundred, or one thousand years hence.

Immortality, in its truest sense, means a state of spiritual
sensibility in which the individual possesses an everlasting, unceasing, consciousness; a mind consciously active, that never
ceases to form thought whether he is asleep or awake. Whether
he inhabits an earthly tabernacle, or has been freed from the
bondage of flesh and clothed in celestial garments, he who has
attained immortality is a dweller in the spiritual realms with
the emancipated sons and daughters of earth, who have passed
on to those higher spheres; there is his real home.

Immortality implies that all the evils incident to earth life,
and also the old accuser that has deceived the human family
from the beginning, have been overcome. It means that the sins
of the past, the sins of omission and commission, have "gone be-

fore him to judgment," and that the individual stands justified
by him who searcheth and knoweth the hearts of all men.   It
means that, although dwelling in a physical form, he, the real
man, is clothed in the spotless garments of spirit; he has been
washed and made clean, he has been born again, not of flesh,
which is corruptible, but of spirit which is incorruptible, which
passes not away but is eternal, being of God, our Creator and
Preserver.   Immortality means that man is filled with the in-
flowing currents of divine life, with the eternal breath of God,
which like a consuming fire burns away the dross, leaving nothing but the purest elements, only those that will withstand the
ravages of time: "and (God) breathed into his nostrils the
breath of life: and man became a living soul."   Genesis II. 7.
The term immortality implies that man has become one with
the Father; he can do nothing of himself, "the Father dwelling
within, he doeth the work."

The great mistake of the Christian church is in believing
that man must die in order to enter into immortal life.   Such a
belief is not only misleading, but it is a barrier to soul growth
and unfoldment.   It is a clog upon man's footsteps, retarding his
progress toward the goal of earthly and spiritual attainment,
and fettering him to a material existence.   It contracts the intellect, dwarfs the understanding, and prevents man from com-
prehending the purpose of the divine Father.   When God
created man, he expressed his purpose in these words, "Let us
make man in our image, after our likeness: and let them have
dominion over the fish of the sea, and over the fowl of the air,
and over the cattle, and over all the earth."   If it is true that
man was created in the image and likeness of God, then it
must follow that, when he has unfolded that likeness, he will
have become immortal and cannot die.   He must live on, ever
growing in spiritual power, until he reaches a period when the
spiritual ego, the real, conscious man, is able to understand the
purpose and will of the divine Father.   Then and not till then
will he be one with the immortals, and, being filled with wisdom

and love, he will be intrusted with spiritual powers which will
not only enable him to say to the elements, "Peace, be still,"
but truthfully to exclaim, "Oh death, where is thy sting? Oh
grave, where is thy victory?"

No man, be he Jew, Christian, Pagan, or Gentile, who passes
into the unseen land through the gateway of the grave, becomes thereby immortal in the true acceptation of the term. The
man whose physical body sees corruption, and becomes food
for worms, is not immortal, no matter what he imagines himself
to be. The man who has not overcome death and the grave is
still mortal; a spiritual soul, clothed it may be in a beautiful
form, with a mind development which makes him a peer among
his fellows, a leader and controller of men, yet he is only a human animal, and cannot express the image in which he was
created. It is sad, nevertheless it is true, that such an one
may pass into the realm of souls with a consciousness of spirit
but a few degrees greater than that possessed by one apparently
far below him in the scale of unfoldment. It frequently occurs
that he does not regain consciousness after the mortal breath
leaves the body. However, the degree of consciousness possessed after death depends entirely upon the degree of recog-
nition given the soul life or consciousness, and its consequent
growth and unfoldment, while on earth. The man who is unconscious after death will remain so until, in the fullness of
time, mother nature awakens him and forces him back into another mortal body, where he will be compelled to take up the
thread of life where it was broken off. The mortal man is
compelled by forcing circumstances to take upon himself a
covering of flesh in order that the expressed purpose of his
Creator may be ultimated. The immortal man who, for a
purpose, desires to return to earth, takes upon himself a body
suited to the needs that bring him among men, and retains it
only as long as he finds a use for it. It is only through rein-
carnation that man gains knowledge enabling him to put off
the mortal and take on the immortal. The purpose underlying

the expulsion of Adam from the garden of Eden was that man might become immortal: when he gains the desired end, he will re-enter the Paradise of God, never again to be driven out.

When the individual has reached that high altitude of soul growth giving him access to the realm of spirit wherein dwell the immortal ones, desires to renounce the fleshly body, he does not lay it in the grave, but, by the power of the Father's will, which has become a part of himself, he commands, " Dust to dust, ashes to ashes, " and, in obedience to the power of the omnipotent word, which is the deific thought from which the spiritual ego has developed, the atoms composing the physical covering separate and return to the source whence they were drawn. The spiritual immortal man, forever free from the thralldom of earthly conditions, passes onward to the realm of the blest, where, the realm in which he shall labor as one of the gods, is determined by USE, the great law of spirit. In the spiritual realm alone, which can only be entered by those who have developed unceasing consciousness, does man enjoy per- -petual youth, being sustained and nourished from that illimit- able fountain of eternal life,—God. He who is able to drink from this everflowing, ever-vivifying, fountain has indeed dis- covered the Elixir of Life, the Philosopher's Stone, which en- ables him to be what he wills to be. Such an one, if he so de- sires, can return to earth as a savior of men. If this is his choice, he must, being superior to the men of earth, walk among them, " treading the wine press alone," unknown, and perhaps despised; yet he is ever conscious of the overshadowing love of his Creator, and can exclaim, as did our Lord and Master, our greatly beloved brother, Jesus the Christ," The Father has not left me alone; for I do always those things that please him."

The Spirit of God never leaves such an one, but in the dark- est hour of trial, when the sins of a perverted world almost crush the sensitive soul, when the bitter cup of trial is placed to the lips, he can, in the solitude of his chamber where adver- saries cannot enter, return to his spiritual home and to those

who know and love him for his great sacrifice, and there receive
the strength to perform his work on earth.   Such an immortal
Son of God, was Jesus, who permitted his body to be laid in
the grave for three days, proving to the world that "the word
became flesh, and dwelt among us,—and we beheld his glory, a
glory of an only-begotten from a father,—full of favor and
truth." (E. G.)   St. John i. 14.

If the man who has gained the pearl of great price, who has
eaten of the fruit of the tree of knowledge of good and evil,
chooses to remain on earth as a server among men, he may do
so: he that is greatest among you, is servant of all.   If this
be his choice he can not only retain his youth and vigor, but he
can keep his mental faculties unimpared: he can even increase his
capacity to understand the laws governing the realm of shadows
called "earth."   He draws his knowledge from the cause realm
which produces all the phenomena witnessed among men.   He
lives entirely on spiritual food, thinks only spiritual thoughts
in harmony with the purpose of God, and, as days succeed
days, his powers increase, until his wisdom transcends the wisdom of men; verily he is no longer a human, but a divine man.
He can, if he so desires, walk the earth a king, a priest unto
God, one with the celestials, not only possessing power over the
things of earth, but also over the unseen forces of nature.

The foregoing statements are based upon knowledge, as well
as upon the assurance of God himself.   In Holy Writ we read,
"But seek ye first the kingdom of God, and his righteousness:
and all these things shall be added unto you."   Matt. vi. 33.
If God commanded man to seek his kingdom, it certainly follows that he can, if he be diligent, find it, for God does not
mock the child he has created.   If it is possible to find the
kingdom of God, it is surely possible to gain immortal life, for
no one can dwell in that kingdom unless all the sins of earth
life have been washed away and a spiritual consciousness gained.
A spiritual consciousness must be an immortal consciousness, as
spirit is eternal.   Again, God is spirit, and only in spirit can

we truly worship him. If, therefore, man does not become
spiritual, which is another term for immortal, he can never gain
heaven, can never worship the Father. Thank God, however,
the way leading to heaven is simple, and easy to find; "the
wayfaring men, though fools, shall not err therein." The purpose in giving these thoughts to the world is to point out the
road that leads from a land of sin, sorrow and death, to one
where death and sorrow cannot enter, but where the Angel of
peace and love rules. The love of the angels will always over-
shadow the sons and daughters of earth who have renounced
the flesh and are seeking immortal life,—oneness with God, the
Father and Creator of the universe.

Until he has paid every debt he owes, the individual must
remain a mortal, must be subject to the law of death and decay, and must continue to return into a fleshly body. If he is
an unjust man, if he loves not his neighbor as himself, if he
takes the name of the Lord in vain, if he bows down to graven
images, if he worships the golden calf, if he is bound by the
physical senses and desires, if his mind is clouded by the passions, he must return to earth, times without number, or until
he has become as pure and innocent as a little babe; it is only
as a little child that he can enter heaven. Heaven is not a
place, but a condition, a state of consciousness; and until he is
able to maintain this heavenly state within himself, man cannot
gain immortality. Until he is able to do so he must earn his
bread in the sweat of his brow, he is still under the law. He
must labor on earth as a mortal until he has unfolded the likeness of God in which he was created. Only after the spirit,
the inner man, gains the dominion over matter is man able to
break the shackles of flesh. Not until then can he stand as a
king, a sovereign having dominion over the old adversary, the
serpent, who has filled our fair earth with sin and error,—the direct cause of misery and death. Man cannot be an immortal, until he is free from the binding and limiting influence of a material
existence; he cannot conquer the power of the grave until he

has obtained control of the forces of nature, which have always compelled the race to be slaves instead of free men.

> "This life's a mystery.
> The value of a thought cannot be told;
> But it is clearly worth a thousand lives
> Like many men's.   And yet men love to live
> As if mere life were worth their living for.
> What but perdition will it be to most?
> Life's more than breath and the quick round of blood
> It is a great spirit and a busy heart.
> The coward and the small in soul scarce do live.
> One generous feeling—one great thought—one deed
> Of good, ere night, would make life longer seem
> Than if each year might number a thousand days,—
> Spent as is this by nations of mankind.
> We live in deeds, not years; in thoughts, not breaths:
> In feelings, not in figures on a dial.
> We should count time by heart-throbs. He most lives
> Who thinks most—feels the noblest—acts the best.
> Life's but a means unto an end—that end,
> Beginning, mean and end to all things—God."

λ

CHAPTER II.

In order to intelligently enter the cause or soul realm it is indispensable that the individual have an understanding of the laws governing that world and the methods of putting himself in harmony with them. As this book is written for general circulation, the necessary explanation will be made in the simplest language possible, and we ask the reader to withhold judgment until he has given them his earnest thought. We promise that if the methods given are faithfully practiced, the results claimed for them certainly will be realized. Should the student fail to realize them, it will not be the fault of the methods, but because of a lack of will and determination on the part of the individual. These laws are God's laws, therefore, they are not subject to change; man is. As he grows in spiritual understanding, he becomes sensitive to the operation of these laws; and, therefore, can readily perceive, obey, and benefit by them. It is for the purpose of giving timely suggestions that we present these methods; and we feel satisfied that, if they are adhered to, the individual will be led to where he need no longer depend upon mortals for instruction and advice. He will be led to where the consciousness of the spiritual ego, will be his consciousness; he will know the relation he bears to the Father, and will, therefore, be in a condition to perceive and comprehend the will and purpose of God concerning him, his mission, and his ultimate destiny; he will be able to draw knowledge from the Mind that controls all the affairs of earth.

Man is threefold in his nature,—body, soul and spirit. To be perfect, an immortal, he must round out all sides of his nature, establishing an equilibrium. Until this result is obtained, he has not reached the goal of human attainment, and is open to various deceptions, and many disappointments. He still lacks wisdom, and is unable to succesfully withstand the subtle forces that guard the spiritual realm from unlawful intruders. It requires a fearless and well-trained will to conquer these monsters who obey only those who have learned how to command them.

The material body of man allies him to the world of effect, which is the visible expression of unseen, and—to the majority of people—unknown laws. These laws are active in the realm of soul, and only a spiritual consciousness is capable of fully understanding them. Man as we know him in our age, does not (appear to) possess this consciousness, at least it is not sufficently active to be of practical use in his daily life. It is latent in all, however, and will manifest itself as soon as the physical body has become sufficiently purified and refined to permit it to do so. We will, therefore, first call attention to the methods by which this much desired condition may be reached.

It is most important that the physical organism be considered: it allies man to the earth, and is the medium through which the soul gains experience and thereby knowledge. The material body is a thought creation, builded of elements drawn from the blood by the Virgo function, the chemist of the human organism. This function is controlled by the intellectual mind, whose seat is in the brain, under orders, as it were, of the soul or interior mind, whose seat is in the Solar Plexus. The body is builded under the direction of the soul mind, in order that it may be a fitting instrument through which the experiences necessary to the soul may be gained.

The man who has not risen above the animal plane requires a material body, in order that he may gain a comprehensive understanding of the laws and methods active in the physical world in which he dwells. The spiritual man requires a more refined organism, in order that he may be able to understand and use the more subtle forces belonging to the realm which he is preparing to enter. The methods by which the body may

be refined and spiritualized are based upon the formulation of
pure and holy thoughts. Before the body can be changed, new
and more refined qualities of life must not only be gathered
but retained in the organism. It is absolutely necessary that
all the life generated by the body be retained, in order that the
blood may be kept filled with the proper magnetic elements
with which to supply to body and mind the vitality required
by all who would withstand the powers of disease and consequent decay.

In order that finer and more spiritual life may be gathered,
more exalted realms of mind must be reached than is possible
or necessary to the man living wholly in the external senses.
This can be accomplished only through soul aspiration, which
is true prayer. This prayer arises in the heart, the seat of the
love nature, the emotions, and the desires. The more exalted
the desire, the higher will be the realm of spirit reached. A
desire to be intelligently formulated must fit some special use
arising in the mind. Holy and unselfish desires bring the
quickest and surest results. If the desire is for an immortal,
spiritual existence, it must be absloutely free from all thought
of self or wish for power to control another. Immortality is
the highest possible attainment man can hope for or at present comprehend, therefore an intelligent desire for such attainment cannot be formulated until the selfhood has been cruci-
fied and forever placed under the absolute control of the higher
faculties of mind.

But one attitude of mind will enable man to reach those
realms of spirit which gives him power with the immortals,
and this mental attitude is not possible until he has grown so
tired of earthly things that he is willing to die to all material
pleasures and desires, hopes and joys. Truly, man must die to
the old before it is possible for him to enter the new; he must
be willing to renounce all ties, of every name and nature, which
in the slightest degree bind him to the old order and condition
of life. He must feel in the interior consciousness that the only

thing which will bring him complete happiness and satisfaction, is to become an instrument in the hands of the Supreme to serve in the elevation of the race to a higher plane of soul consciousness.

The man who would become an immortal must truly desire to be a servant of humanity. To attain this end he must first know himself: he must be able to analyze every desire arising in the heart, to decide whether it is useful to his welfare or a hindrance to his spiritual progress. The desires must be controlled by the mind. Use must be the law governing his actions. He must be able to utilize or reject any or all of his desires and emotions. Not only must he be able to do this, but he must be willing to place himself, without a doubt or reservation, in the keeping of his highest conception of God; he must be willing absolutely to trust his heavenly Father, whose wisdom, love, and justice, he knows will permit only only those trials and disappointments that are necessary to his welfare.

Two ways of living are presented to all; man can, if he so desires, rely upon his own strength, or upon the power of the Spirit. If his dependence is in the power of flesh, he trusts in human judgment, which is unreliable. If he is satisfied to depend upon the power of the Spirit to guide, he will always have a sure refuge in the hour of need. If he must still lean upon the uncertain arm of flesh, if it is impossible for him to trust God wholly, he cannot obtain the guidance of the Spirit. When man can trust God fully, the power of the Father is his; he is in a condition to enter the "Narrow Way," the way of holiness. And if he unfaulteringly treads the way of holiness, he will soon realize that sorrow and pain have fled, never to return—and they never will return unless he wanders from the true path. Every mortal that would leave the land of shadow, must tread the "Narrow Way" of holiness. It is the only way by which the land of eternal sunshine can be reached.

No dangers or trials are ever found in the Way of Holiness.

But he who strays from the true path, because of striving to live up to his own ideals, will find himself confronted by difficulties and dangers. To keep in the path is to be ever conscious of the presence of the Spirit. Live rightly, regardless of what it costs. To follow the inner promptings of the soul, without reference to the opinion of others, is the only safe way. Patience and fortitude of soul is, therefore, to be learned here; no matter what may come to you, do not falter, but with renewed energy, determination, and prayer, press onward; you can, and eventually will, if you are faithful, reach the desired haven.

Many grand and devout souls are scattered throughout the land, who continually think pure and holy thoughts, and who daily pray, "Let thy kingdom come, thy will be done," yet apparently they do not obtain an answer to their prayer. They live, perhaps, the allotted three score years and ten, and pass from earth without reaching the goal of earthly existence. They fail to reach that goal because they have no knowledge of the law, therefore do not live in obedience to it. These beautiful souls are God's little, well beloved children. Their prayers, when truly from the soul, have been always answered; perhaps not as they hoped, but, nevertheless, answered. Such souls are tenderly nurtured and protected by our ever watchful, loving Parent. Whenever he sees that the experience necessary to fit them for future use has been obtained, he gathers them to himself. These grand souls must, however, re-incarnate, and again become workers among men. They will not remember the past, but their aspirations and devout, unselfish life, have builded beautiful and highly exalted souls. Thousands of such are active members in the Christian churches, awaiting the time when God sees fit to awaken them to their true use in his vineyard.

The souls now on earth who are ready to comprehend God's laws are no longer little children; they have grown to be men and women. Therefore God no longer carries them in his bosom, with jealous love protecting and guarding them from

all dangers, but sets them upon their feet, and gives the command, "Go work in my vineyard." They have grown old
enough to be trusted with the mysteries of life, and of death.
The proof of their readiness is in the deep yearning of the soul
to know the will of the Father that they may do it. They
could but imperfectly obey the will before, because they had
not the necessary experience. They could not dedicate their
all to the Father, because they were unable to comprehend the
need of such a renunciation. They could not take the name of
God for their protection, because they did not know his name.
(The name and its use will be explained further on.)

If our readers have reached a mature stage of growth, they
will understand the need of a complete surrender to the Spirit
of God. Feeling the necessity of this is not sufficient; the surrender must be made by the interior nature, by every atom of
the being. Years of constant effort are required, and much
self-sacrifice, before this most desirable end can be fully realized. The old ego, self, continually present, is an almost insurmountable barrier to the unfoldment of soul powers. It
stands ever beside man to remind him of his earthly existence,
and, as it is the personality, it will not be set aside without a
great struggle. Self dies hard, and dies only after the inner
man has gained complete mastery over the lower nature. If
you would set aside the lower self and replace it by the spiritual man, the celestial-born son of God, you must avoid those
who scoff at sacred, or spiritual things. Seek only the society
of those who are pure and free from sensual thoughts. It
would be far better to dwell in solitude than to spend your time
in the company of the ungodly.

The man who would reach the high goal of human attainment, oneness with God, must learn not to condemn his fellows. He should look upon man as a creation of God, and as
possessing the latent powers of an archangel. There is good
in all; search for the good, and ever love the divine principle,
hidden, it may be, under a rough and repulsive exterior. Overcome evil with good. Pray constantly that you may receive

from God, wisdom, knowledge, and understanding. Remember, however, that you will not receive these gifts until you have renounced evil and are able to hold fast to the good. Only those who are able to discreetly use divine wisdom will receive it into their hearts. Without wisdom from on high, you will surely fail in your struggle to overthrow the powers of evil which have heretofore controlled your life.

If man would throw off the mortal and put on the immortal, he must not attempt to store up riches in provision for the future. Such an attitude of mind, in itself, precludes the possibility of gaining an immortal existence. Remember that the man or the woman who has renounced the world, who has dedicated his or her life to God, no longer owns that life, but must live up to the injunction of Jesus, "Take no thought for the morrow: for the morrow shall take thought for the things of itself. Sufficient unto the day is the evil thereof." Matt. vi. 34. (Carefully consider St. Matthew, VI.) If your dedication has been complete, you will know that God has accepted you, and that he will provide all things necessary to your comfort. It is not to be inferred, as many will undoubtedly do, that you are to sit down in idleness, depending upon God to bring you the needed supplies in some miraculous manner. Such a course will surely bring disappointment; God will do nothing for you that you can do yourself. It is only the unbalanced man, the man lacking in knowledge and understanding, who trusts in this way. The wise man, the well-balanced son of God, does his best, and when he has done this, he confidently, with loving trust, looks to his Father, knowing full well that, when the limit of his own strength has been reached, God will supply that which is lacking.

The man who would receive the illumination of the Spirit, must use whatever mind power he may possess; it is only through use that such faculties are developed. Therefore he must continually gather thought, not alone for his own need, but for the needs of those who stand below him in soul unfoldment. As he gathers and disseminates this vital thought, clothed with the potential energies drawn from the mind of God, his mind quickens into greater action, and, in consequence, becomes more receptive, or better able to reflect the purpose of the higher mind and will. The more you give, the more you will receive: the more unselfish you are, the more perfectly will you be able to gather thoughts that will be of benefit to others.

We advise those who are seeking immortality to cast their bread upon the waters, to scatter it upon the tide of human life. Rest assured, if you do so, with the desire active to serve the needs of humanity, it will return, increased an hundred fold. Neither the man who tries to obtain knowledge for self alone, nor the one who sits down and dreams his time away, will amount to very much: both will slowly but surely sink into that state of sleep which means, not immortality but death — death not only to the physical man, but to the mental as well. The dreamer will never reach the high goal of attainment, he will never enter heaven: only the fearless, unselfish warrior who is constantly on the alert, ever watching the enemy in order to gain the mastery over it, will obtain the right to dwell in the kingdom of the blest.

The man who dreams instead of laboring, has the opportunity for soul growth presented to him, but as he sleeps, he does not perceive it. If he gathers thoughts at all, they are not practical. Not having his purpose well defined, he has no center from which to work, no foundation upon which to erect his spiritual structure. He is like a ship without a chart or compass. When the dark tempestuous night overtakes the dreamer, he will awaken to find himself struggling upon the quicksand of doubt and materialism, lost through disobedience and wasted opportunities. The man who dreams instead of laboring, weakens his mental faculties, and therefore becomes an easy prey to the vampires who feed upon humanity. His struggles are of short duration, however; he soon passes from earth to enter the land of souls, not as immortal, but as one in a dream, continually lamenting his wasted opportunities, his misspent life, un-

til kind nature puts him to sleep, a state in which he remains
until the time arrives for him to again take on an earthly covering, to begin life where he left off, with greater trials before
him than he has yet encountered.

The idle dreamer is of but little use to the human race. Instead of building upon the only sure foundation,—the rock of
truth,—a tower whose light will illuminate the earth, he builds
upon the sands of uncertainty, and never really lays the foundation for a well-balanced spiritual nature. If you would be an
overcomer of evil, if you would command and be obeyed, you
must labor incessantly with your body and with your mental
faculties: labor with the body in order that it may be filled with
enduring strength and vigor; labor with your mental faculties in
order that, through use, you may so develop them that the power
of man be transformed into the transcendental power of a god.
The mental faculties are the servants of the spirit, and through
them you receive spiritual illumination. Mind is all that sur-
vives when the external covering is cast off. Therefore, if you
would unfold that consciousness that never slumbers or sleeps,
use every means at your command. When you do this, higher
means will be presented to you, and in time you will realize
in every fiber of your being that you have truly passed from
death unto life; not through the gateway of the grave, but
through the alliance of your finite mind to the infinite mind
of God.

CHAPTER III.

In the preceding chapter we stated that, by a process of the mind, the material body is builded of thought potencies drawn from elements of life contained in the blood. If the seeker after immortality would have a physical organism that is proof against the adversaries disease and death, and one able freely to supply the demands of the mind, he must keep it filled with the elements of life. Those living in the old order of life cannot do this; the life generated is not all retained, as it should be, but is continually being squandered in the gratification of abnormal passions, the natural fruit of ignorance and unrestrained animal desires. Squandering the precious elements of life, causes an abnormal drain upon the fountain of supply; this weakens the organs which gather, and, as they become impotent, they are unable to perform the task imposed upon them. As the supply diminishes, youthful vivacity and vigor are superseded by old age, and death finally results.

Once in every four weeks there is born within the human organism a germ, designated a "psychic germ." This germ is endowed with higher qualities of life than are the germs from which the physical body has been builded, and which are generated daily. It may be called the "evolutionary germ," for through the potencies of the life contained in it man advances toward his ultimate destiny, oneness with Spirit. When limited, or incorporated into form, be it animal or human, life always struggles to express the qualities of mind with which it is endowed; consequently, as the life contained in a psychic germ is endowed with mental power beyond that possessed by the individual, and as it endeavors to express that higher quality, manifestly a struggle is the result. As the mind strives to harmonize the body, and to adjust it to the more spiritual potencies with which it has been entrusted, a state of mental antagonism arises; so that if the mind is not centralized on spirit, and if it is not free from sense desire, the struggles result in the vital, spiritual germ being rejected from the organism.

The loss of the spiritual germ generally occurs during sleep, when the mind is passive and unconscious of the needs of the physical body. The time of the birth of this germ is governed by the moon, and it is qualitated by the astral ether in which that body is at the time immersed. Each month, as the moon enters the sign in which the earth was at the birth of the individual, a psychic germ is born. If this germ is retained in the organism until the moon enters the sign it occupied at birth, the germ is transmuted, and its mind qualities become incorporated into the man. This higher and more spiritual life increases the physical and mental capacity of the individual. If the psychic germ be transmuted, the next germ is born one sign earlier, and is qualitated by the ether in which the moon is at that time. · This process continues until the qualities of the twelve signs are incorporated into the organism. When the twelve qualities have become thus incorporated, the powers of the earth's zodiac are at the command of the student. The second cycle of twelve gives him the powers of the sun's zodiac.

The vital, or psychic germs are the twelve manner of fruit growing upon the tree of life which produces fruit once a month. Through the incorporation of spiritual germs into the organism man gradually develops beyond the influence of the planets,—a condition which is obtained when he evolves into, and lives from, the grand solar zodiac. As it takes over 2,000 years to pass through one sign of the grand solar zodiac, and as the qualities received from it are wholly spiritual, his entrance into this zodiac marks the time when the student becomes free from earthly conditions and starts upon that journey of celestial development which knows no end. Thus his growth is eternal, his power to gain and utilize knowledge knows no limit, and,

as he advances toward spirit, the greatest joy of his existence
will be in the realization of the fact, that, in the unnumbered
ages to come, he still will be only on the borderland of the il-
limitable universe that God has created, and permits man to
explore.

The unrestrained gratification of the sense desires results in
abnormal passions, which dull the finer sensibilities, benumb
the mental faculties, cause man to squander the precious fluid
of life, and so corrupt his mind that he is almost wholly governed by a distorted imagination. This lusting after the flesh,
has so blunted his higher nature as to have almost deprived
him of the finer spiritual instinct, or intuitions, which are the
only sure guide to health and contentment. It has caused him
to become so immersed in material substance, that he has lost
sight of the true use for which the "power of creation" was
given him. Such a course of life produces in the interior nature a condition of unrest and dissatisfaction, which results directly in unhappiness, disease, and death.

The lower animals, being absolutely controlled by the creative mind which rules the forces of generation, obey implicitly
the prompting of nature, which is, "Increase and multiply, and
replenish the earth." Man alone misuses the powers intrusted
to him, and we find the fruits of his sin filling our jails, pen-
itentiaries, and asylums with beings in human form, indeed,
but with instincts far below those of their brothers who find
embodiment in brute form. The sin of the parents finds expression through their children, producing, in many instances,
such abnormal desires, that, even in childhood, they are frequently enslaved by those vices which rob man of his true
manly dignity and godlikeness.

Refusing to resist unholy desire, and, on the other hand,
seeking pleasure in order to gratify the lustings of the lower
nature, have so weakened the will of man as to make it almost
impossible for him to resist these lustings. The end of such a
course of life is fearful to contemplate—a day of reckoning

must surely come. The gratification of unholy desire is the direct cause of sin, is the main spring of all the evils which causes such dark shadows to envelop our race. The man who makes no effort to control his sense nature is very low in spiritual unfoldment. In his insane desire to satisfy the awful craving of the senses, he tramples in the dust all the holier instincts of the refined and virtuous. Such depravity, if permitted to continue, must, sooner or later, bring ruin and disaster to the human race.

The abnormal craving and gratification of sense desire have created in the unseen world monsters of most malignant character. These creations of unholy passion are inflamed and controlled by lustful cravings that nothing will appease. Creations of inharmonious and perverted thought, formed by a mind governed by unrestrained passion, and depending on the over-flow of human life to sustain their consciousness * and to gain power, these creatures become vampires haunting the borderland in order to prey upon humanity. They know no distinction of persons, no one is free from their baneful presence. They haunt the chambers of the pure as well as those of the impure, but prefer the impure, because the depraved are more in sympathy with themselves: no one, however, is entirely free from their evil influence. They delight in darkness and sin, and prey upon their unconscious victims during both the waking and sleeping state. During sleep they reflect the most depraved and lustful thoughts upon the mind, causing dreams of such a nature that the dreamer looses the divine, life-creating, and life-sustaining substance while he is unconscious, and therefore unable to protect himself.

Physicians, parents, priests, and scientists, who should be true advisers and spiritual guides, delude humanity with the idea that the loss of the vital fluid is not only necessary to health, but conducive to mental strength as well. They claim

*Many will question this assertion, but from personal observation the author is convinced that the human elemental does depend upon human life to perpetuate its consciousness.

that loss of the seminal fluid during sleep cannot be controlled,
that it is nature's method of relieving the system of the surplus
accumulation of life, which otherwise would produce disease and
seriously affect the organism.   Such ideas are not only repulsive to the finer instincts of man, but are erroneous in the ex-
treme. This perverted and unnatural belief, so prevalent among
the masses, and the criminal neglect on the part of parents,
who refuse, through false modesty, to impart the needed instructions to their offspring, has produced a most deplorable
state of morals in the social world; such a state, in fact, as
makes it almost impossible for the spiritual man to exist on
earth at the present time, and tens of thousands of the fairest,
purest, and most spiritual, the choicest flowers that God has
planted in this world of matter, early fade and die, simply because they cannot live in the hotbed of vice which it has become.   These beautiful souls, who so early pass from the trials
and sorrows of earth life, are true saviors. Could they live and
mature, could their holy thoughts and aspirations find lodgment in the hearts of men, a great change would soon take
place; men would quickly learn that the ways of God lead to
happiness and joy, that the tree of knowledge does indeed
bring forth immortal fruit, does indeed impart wisdom and understanding to all who, through purity of desire, are enabled
to eat of it.

As our earth grows older, sin, sorrow, and unrest increase,
until there is scarcely a contented and thoroughly happy individual to be found.   There must be a cause for this, otherwise
such conditions would not exist; and the cause undoubtedly lies
in the fact that the distorted condition of mind, caused by a
depraved and uncontrolled use of the sex nature, has forced
man from the path marked out for him by our all-wise and
loving Creator.   He has wandered so far from the true path
that he has lost sight of the the purpose for which he was created.   He has become so thoroughly steeped in the material
elements of earth that he has forgotten, or, if he has not for-

gotten, he is unable to use, his spiritual powers. These powers are, however, still latent within, and can be again used, as they were before the fall of man when Adam walked and talked with God. As man was created in order that he might be the means through which the Creator could manifest his wondrous power and love, and as man has gained sufficient knowledge to enable him to do this, the present condition of disease and consequent unrest can exist but a short time longer.

Man was permitted to fall from the high spiritual state in which he once existed, in order that he might have knowledge requisite to command the principalities and powers of the universe. He has now gained sufficient soul powers to do this; although. at present, they lay dormant, awaiting the inflow of divine love to quicken them to action. These powers will quickly spring into manifestation, however, when the earthly tabernacle has been cleansed. freed from those evils which sap, and eventually destroy, the higher faculties. Those who are striving after an immortal existence, will find that a task appalling to a Hercules is before them, when they thus try to cleanse the tabernacle. As they begin to inspire the elements of spirit they will become conscious that the depraved state of the human mind has produced such gross conditions in the atmosphere, that only the most depraved and vicious can exist with any degree of comfort and happiness. The spiritual man or woman will soon realize that, if he or she would worship God after the dictates of the heart, there is no place on earth in which to do so, no atmosphere that is untainted with the lustful emanations of a sinful people, apparently no sphere of mind from which to draw pure and holy thought.

The man who is beginning to overcome his lower nature, and who realizes that he is living in and surrounded by impure and baneful influences, must not despair and return to the old condition; there is a sphere from which to breathe, as well as a realm of thought as pure as when it was created by our Father, who knows perfectly the needs of his children; there is a relam

of mind and life-sustaining elements that the lustful thoughts
and desires of man cannot penetrate. All may reach this
realm, and, by the powers of God unfolded within them,
they may draw therefrom, not only pure and immortal life
qualities, but elements of mind which will illuminate the brain
to such a degree of intensity that the thoughts created no
longer partake of the crude, uncertain form of a material existence, but, being clothed in elements undefiled, are robed in
the spiritual garment of truth. It takes a strong and determined effort, together with an intense yearning of the interior,
on the part of the seeker after truth, if he would know God, if
he would reach beyond the environments of earth and draw,
from the fountains of divine, immortal life, the pure elements
needed to sustain and nourish the spiritual man, the human being who has become the divine son of God.

In the ages that have long since faded from the minds of men,
when our earth was young and undefiled by the base passions of
animal humanity, the way to the higher realms, "was broad and
free from trial, and brought immortal fruit; but when Adam
fell, the way became narrow and full of dangers." It is very
different in our age, as the seeker after an immortal existence
will realize before he has gone far. The monsters that have
been created by man,—man as an individual and as a race,—
the spirits that control the elements, as well as those that find
a home within the individual, must be met, and conquered by
him. The misshapen entities which live in the borderland sepa-
rating the two worlds, must be made servants to your will, my
reader, before they will permit you to pass beyond their kingdom.
The creative word, the spirit that controls generation in all its
varied forms, and compels all nature to reproduce each after
its kind, must be made obedient to your command. This is
not possible until the likeness of the Father manifests itself in
you. You must be proven and tried to your utmost capacity
of endurance; you must wrestle with the god of nature (The
Elohim), even as Jacob the patriarch of old did. And when

you realize, as he did, that you are indeed a conqueror, you will comprehend many of the mysteries veiled from sinful man, and will understand that Jacob's vision was not a creation of his imagination, for the angels of the Lord will descend and bless you as they did him. They will feed you with the heavenly manna, of which the mortal unregenerated man can know nothing.

The Herculean task which lies before all those who would gain immortality would be utterly impossible of accomplishment by mortal man, were it not for the fact that God has promised that if you dedicate your life to him, you will be his sons, and he will be your strength. A dedication of your life to God and a renunciation of self, is absolutely necessary to a realization of this promise. "Ye shall have no other power beside me," was the command of God to ancient Israel, and, in so far as they kept the covenant, he was indeed their strength. Other gods and powers beside the God of creation have heretofore ruled your lives. If you would become immortal, you must refuse to serve the powers of evil; your trust must no longer be in man, in the gods of gold and silver, but in the Supreme Ruler of all, our hope and our strength.

The seeker after immortality, after the dedication to God has been determined upon, must live a life of absolute purity, a life of celibacy; nay, more, a life of absolute continency, a life free from every desire for sense gratification of any name or nature. He has entered the eternal sabbath and must cease from the work of creation,—generation,—as did God when he finished his labors. Without a single reservation, he must fully determine in the interior that all the life gathered shall be wholly devoted to the use of the body and mind. He must dedicate that life to the higher uses of spiritual unfoldment, and, by constant prayer and holy desire, so impregnate his entire being with holy and righteous thought, that he may become filled with spiritual light and power. The monsters, the creations of a mind governed by lust, dread the light, and cannot approach

or torment the individual who is consecrated to God and has
become illuminated by the inflow of the diviner elements of
spirit. "For thou wilt light my candle: the Lord my God will
enlighten my darkness." Psalms XVIII. 28.

Beginners will find great difficulty in conserving all the life
gathered; many years of constant effort are frequently required
to accomplish the desired results. But the waste of life must
be controlled, otherwise immortality is impossible. Constant
vigilance and unyielding determination must be ever active;
you must continually remain in the watch tower. Refuse to
allow impure thoughts to find a lodgment in the mind. Your
desires must be entirely free from all those things which, in any
way, ally you to the world of generation. Your association
with the opposite sex must be of such a character as to pre-
clude all desire for carnal relation. You must avoid those who
are impure in thought, word, or act. If the presence of any person
causes you to have unholy desires, avoid that person as you would
a pestilence. Do not lose sight of the fact that you can commit
adultery in thought as well as act. "Sing, O barren, thou that
didst not bear; break forth into singing, and cry aloud, thou
that didst not travail with child: for more are the children of
the desolate than the children of the married wife, saith the
Lord." Isa. LIV.1. The waking thoughts follow man into the
dream state, and if he indulges in impure thoughts, they will
cause dreams that will bring regrets and disappointment.

The mind governs the physical body in the sleeping as it does
in the waking state. If it is unhampered by astral influences
or other causes, it will guard the body and prevent loss of the
vital fluid, as the sleeping as well as the waking consciousness
obeys only the promptings of the Spirit to whom the individual
has dedicated his life. You must not depend upon the Spirit to
overcome for you; if you do so, you will surely be disappointed.
You must overcome for yourself, by your own strength; the
Spirit supplies power only when you have done your utmost to
overcome. It is an easy matter to control the life fluids while

the body is active and all the faculties are on the alert; but
during sleep, when the faculties are passive, the great difficulty
arises.   The soul never sleeps; and, if you would control the
body during the hours of rest, you should, when retiring, impress upon the soul by means of auto-suggestion the imperative
necessity of remaining with the body to protect it.   The subjective consciousness, the soul, obeys the mandate of the objective consciousness, the mind, if the will is sufficiently strong to
enforce obedience.   If the will be kept active by persistent effort, it will in time grow strong enough to accomplish this purpose.   As the energies are stored, and as the mental and physical body becomes refined, the dead, unconscious sleep gradually ceases.   As man becomes conscious of his spiritual nature,
he loses all desire for unconscious sleep; when he lays the body
down to rest, he passes from a lower state of consciousness to a
higher, but he never permits the action of the interior mind to
cease.   You must strive by all the methods at your command
to cease from that sleep which is death.   When you retire at
night, after you have impressed the soul with the command "Be
watchful," commence a line of thought, and endeavor, with the
interior mind, to hold to it without wavering.   Your first attempt may not be entirely successful; after some months, however, if you are persistent and are able to conserve the vital
fluids, you will notice a gradual change, hardly perceptible at
first, but, if you hold fast to your purpose, complete success
will crown your efforts.   When you have overcome the old unconscious sleep, you will have developed the ability to perceive
and understand the mysteries of the soul realm.   As the subject of sleep is a very important one, we will elaborate upon
it further on.

The student who does not at first succeed in retaining the
vital fluids, must not be discouraged.   If failures occur, there
is still some mental reservation, some desire for sense gratification, remaining hidden in some recess of the mind.   Search dili-
gently, until the difficulty has been found and cast out.   The

dominion can never be obtained until all desire for sense gratification has been destroyed.   The dominion over the monsters
who haunt your chamber will never be gained until the mind
is in perfect accord with the purpose of the higher self, which
is complete emancipation from all carnal lusts and desires. As
man succeeds in transmuting the vital fluids, his consciousness
increases, and the organism becomes more receptive to spiritual
impressions; his intuitonal, or interior powers increase to a
marvelous degree, until, as time rolls on, his exterior and interior consciousness become one. When the union of the higher
and lower self takes place, you will have a consciousness that
rests not day nor night, but ever increases in its power of action and continually draws you closer to God, until eventually
you can truly say, as did our Lord, "I and my Father are one,"
which is the ultimate destiny of all men.

    In striving to overcome all waste of the vital fluid, man
must be ever on his guard against doing those things that will
weaken the normal action of the organs of sex. The idea is,
not to destroy or weaken in any way, but to build up and
strengthen. The normal activity of the sex, especially in the
early morning hours, is caused by the fires that are transmuting the gross material substance to finer and more spiritual
ones. This activity must not be suppressed, nature must not
be interfered with in her endeavors to work in harmony with
God's laws. While the fires of transmutation are active, the
mind should be not only absolutely free from lustful thoughts,
but, in loving aspiration and with the soul open to receive the
inflow of his Spirit, it should be centralized on God, the source
of all life and power. At this time, if the right attitude of
mind be held, the fires of God will descend and fill the individual with love and peace. These fires consume the dross, leaving only the purer elements, which strengthen and enrich the
blood, illuminate the intellect, and truly give man access to the
fountains of living waters, that wash away all taint of death
and decay. This inflow of divine fire is the true elixir of life,

sought for by many, but gained by only the few exalted, illuminated seers who have willingly surrendered the vanities and
delusions of earth life, in order that they may be worthy to enter the kingdom of God, where alone will be found the bread
of life which endows man with not only an immortal consciousness, but with knowledge enabling him to fathom mysteries
wisely hidden from all those who are controlled by depraved
and soul-destroying sense desires.

CHAPTER IV.

It should be borne in mind that each individual is endowed with characteristics and requirements peculiarly his own; therefore in their practical application, these instructions may be modified to suit the needs of the student. The writer has presented only such methods as have been successfully applied by his associates and which he has found adapted to his own peculiar requirements. In order to obtain the most speedy and lasting results, the student should make a careful study of his individual needs. If he does so, he will soon be able to mark out for himself the course of life best adapted to hasten the unfoldment of the powers of his soul; and, as he advances, he will be able to make such changes in these methods as will suit the requirements of his individual organism. He should be careful, however, not to develop one side of his nature at the expense of another; in order to be practical man must have all sides of his nature equally unfolded, therefore great care should be exercised, or evil results may follow the application of these methods. Be sure not to misinterpret our words, as many will do. If we advise the "conservation of the life," we mean absolute conservation. If we recommend total renunciation of the "material things of earth," we wish you to understand us as meaning that it must be done without a single reservation. Many believe that they are living the life of regeneration, when they are far from doing so. Such will never obtain the results promised. The fault lies with the individual and not with the methods of life recommended. Remember the words of Jesus: "No man can serve two masters: * * * ye cannot serve God and mammon."

The character of the perfect man is so well balanced in its

unfoldment that all sides of his nature work together without friction, in complete harmony with the design of God. Unless this condition obtains, immortality is impossible; the Spirit will be unable to express its divine likeness. The man who would obtain and retain perfect health, and consequent happiness, must have the physical organism under perfect control. He must be master in the house he occupies, and in which he gains an understanding of law that enables him to become a creator, a king, a son of God. If the physical body is not under control of the higher faculties, unclean spirits will enter and defile this temple of the soul. A diseased body is conclusive evidence that the mind controlling it is not working in harmony with the interior man, or in accordance with law. The interior man will forever remain earth-bound, unless it awakens to its true nature and requirements. When it thus awakens, it will build a physical organism that will be free from the possibilities of disease and death, and through which it can express its divine power.

Before the interior man can gain complete control over its physical organism, it must realize that it is spirit, it must become fully conscious that the external body is only an instrument builded of material elements by the mind, which is under direction to serve the needs of the soul. Such thoughts as "I am spirit;" I live from the Father, therefore "I am perfect;" "I cannot die," should be impressed upon the consciousness until they are fully realized in every fiber of the being. If these thoughts are held in the mind, and not a doubt is allowed to enter, "faith" is awakened in the individual, a mental state inherited from the "word of God," the power of creation, or generation, which governs the life of the planet earth. When an immortal man determines to perform certain acts, the power of "faith" enables him to say, without fear of failure, "It shall be done," and the desired results are obtained. Without this inherent power, which is termed "faith," and which must not be confounded with "belief," man could not exist for a sin-

gle moment. When he reaches the point where he realizes that
"he is one with the Father," he will be able to draw the power
of faith into his organism from the Source of all power, and the
measure of the inspiration will be limited only by his needs.
Jesus said, "If ye have faith as a grain of mustard seed, ye
shall say unto this mountain, Remove hence to yonder place;
and it shall remove: and nothing shall be impossible unto you."
Matt. XVII. 20.   The full meaning of "faith" can neither be
expressed nor understood by a man living wholly in the intellect.   If intellectual man were able to understand this mysterious, spiritual, and irresistible force, he would be possessed of
powers that he could not handle, and which would prove his
destruction; therefore our Father has, in his great wisdom, hidden it from the wise ones of earth, but will reveal it to the
spiritual babes who are one with Christ. We can, at best, only
hope to lead the student to where he will be able to gain through
his own interior comprehension, an understanding of this most
subtle power which God has implanted within all. We can perceive how it is manifested in vegetable, animal, and human life,
but the mysterious law which governs it will remain unformu-
lated by the human mind until man reaches the sublime degree
of spirit consciousness. St. Paul defines faith as "the substance
of things hoped for, the evidence of things not seen." Hebrews
II. 1.   Faith has a part in all life upon our planet, from the
lowest to the highest. Without faith the grass could not grow,
and man himself, were he entirely devoid of faith, would be
unable to perform the simplest act, even to the moving of a
muscle. This faith, which St. Paul wisely terms "the substance
of things hoped for," can be increased in man, providing he
dedicates his life unreservedly to God and trusts him without
a doubt.   When he can do this, he will be able, by the power
of soul prayer, to draw this substance into his organism; and
then he will always have the support of the strong arm of the
Father.   He will no longer be compelled to depend upon the
arm of flesh; his help and defense will be in the God of the
universe.

The will of man is the epitome of his mind force, or power of action. It is the sum total of the strength possessed by the mind to decree, and to carry to ultimates the purpose of that decree. An unyielding will is an absolute necessity to those who are striving to overcome the power of the grave; for without it they will be unable to conquer the adversaries that use every means to prevent them from gaining power and dominion over death. These adversaries know that when a man has become immortal, all beneath him is subject to his desires. The will may be strengthened by continually holding to the thought, "I will succeed." Will to do only those things that you feel you have the power to accomplish; otherwise you will weaken instead of strengthen your will.

Begin the work of strengthening the will by taking complete control of the physical body. Man, being the epitome of the whole, will find that, when he has gained full control of his own organism, he has gained control of the forces outside of himself. Should the body feel dull and refuse to perform the duties assigned to it, compel it to do so. If it is in pain, refuse to be misled; endeavor to realize in every fiber of your being, that you are spirit, therefore cannot suffer, and move steadily forward, refusing to be bribed either by pain or pleasure. If the appetite craves food that you know will deaden the sensibilities and will not nourish the body, refuse to eat it. Great discretion must be used in the care of the body. It would be impossible for us to specify a line of dietetics; that which would be "meat to one, would be poison to another." If wisdom is used in the matter of food,—eating to live, not living to eat,— a normal appetite will soon be acquired, which will at all times be a certain guide. However, we do recommend abstinence from spices, tea, coffee, tobacco, and alcohol. After you have gained complete control of the lower nature, you will understand where St. Paul stood when he said, "All things are lawful unto me, but all things are not expedient: all things are lawful for me, but I will not be brought under the power of

any." I. Cor. vi. 12. You must remember that in your struggle to overcome passion you will have all that you can possibly
do, therefore you should avoid all those things that will in any
way stimulate or increase the power of the old serpent. Look
upon the body simply as an animal; attend to its needs, but
nothing more. You will find, after you have shut off the waste
of the life, that you require very little food. If you feel the
need of stimulants, draw what you require from the fountain
of life, to which you have free access. If you ignore the senses,
and look upon them as only servants given by an all-wise Creator for the purpose of apprising you of the needs of the physical body, you will quickly develop the stoic, and be able to
decide for yourself as to both the amount and quality of food
you require.

There are two kinds of will,—the will of energy and the
will of stillness. The will of energy actuates the physical body
and enables the student to gain control of external conditions.
The will of stillness is the interior or spiritual will; it works in
silence as does the will of God. It is the latter will that enables man to be a creator, to command the forces and elements
of nature; through its power man is able to pierce further and
further into spirit, until he stands before the great white throne,
and becomes a "pillar in the temple of his God." We see the
power of this will manifested in the silence of nature; in the
growing grass, the budding trees, the blooming flowers. All
nature lives and grows under the command of this resistless
force. It would be well for the seeker after truth to remember
that silence does much to unfold the consciousness of the soul;
"Be still and know God," is a wise command. It is only in the
stillness of the soul, in the sacred center of being, where the
flame burns steadily upon the altar, that God's presence is felt
and his voice heard. The literal rendering of the word "sin,"
is noise, confusion; it therefore follows that, if man would grow
in wisdom and be free from sin, he should dwell as much as
possible in silent musing. It is also true that the more highly

developed the soul, the greater the love for the silence, the more intense the desire to be free from the noise and confusion of the world, to dwell with God in the realm of silence. The prophet Jeremiah advises, "Let us enter into the defensed city, and let us be silent there." Jer. VIII. 14. We also, dear reader, advise you to learn to be silent, if you desire wisdom and the guidance of God.

The wills may be strengthened and made to work in their specific fields of service by the following drills: In the seclusion and silence of your chamber, quietly sit with your face toward the east, body erect, and hands placed lightly upon the knees. Endeavor to realize the fact that you are in the life currents of the Infinite, to whom your life has been dedicated. Let your mind go out to Him in loving trust and desire that your body may be filled with those qualities of his life which are necessary to the ultimation of the purpose to which your life has been consecrated. Breathe slowly and regularly, in the following manner:—As you draw in the breath, pronounce the word WILL, mentally, and as you exhale the breath, pronounce the word STILL, also mentally. As the breathing is continued you will draw in the qualities of life you require, it being a law that we always draw to us those things which we truly desire from the soul. This manner of sitting and breathing makes you receptive to the inflow of divine life. Sit for at least fifteen minutes daily; thirty minutes would be better, but in the beginning the student is apt to relax his vigilance, and under such circumstances evil results may follow. Be careful not to fall asleep during your time of sitting, as to do so places you in danger of being obsessed by those adversaries who are drawn to you at this time, and who will endeavor to turn you from your purpose. Be negative to the mind and will of God, and positive to all other influences. Sit for a purpose, clear and well defined. Should visions of any character come before the mind, set them aside; one thing at a time should be an unfailing rule.

The masters,—those who have become immortal, and who

have passed beyond physical environments, are the only ones
recognized by the writer as masters,—will always render assist-
ance to those who are endeavoring to strengthen the will by
lawful methods and for a wise purpose. The student who desires help from these wise and holy men should remember that
egotism is not will. The line between the consciousness of your
superior endowments—gained by living a life of renunciation
and regeneration—and egotism, is so narrow that few have the
power of discrimination sufficiently developed to define it. It
is right and proper for you to recognize your divine sonship,
but you should at the same time remember that you are still a
babe, still swayed by the passions, still human, still under the
law of sin and death. To rise above that law you must always
hold the spirit of love and charity toward all God's creatures.
Should you imagine that you are specially favored of God because of your personality, you will retard your advancement;
and should you hold to this error, you will fall, never to rise
again in this incarnation—"God is no respecter of persons."
As you continue to live in harmony with the expressed purpose
of the Father, and to develop the diviner principles, you will
draw closer to him, and be better able to express diviner attributes than can those who have not the soul unfoldment that
you possess; but at the same time remember that the spirit
which animates all men is equal; that all, in time, will reach
oneness with God, and will, therefore, become the perfect expression of principles. It is man's nearness to God, which
alone makes him superior to his fellows. If you are superior
your life will be marked by deeds of charity and love, unselfish
acts, and freedom from those vices which benumb the higher
faculties. Never use the power of your will to control the actions of another; to do so is to commit one of the worst crimes
possible to imagine. God has given every man the right to the
unrestrained use of his mentality, and should you in any way
endeavor to control the mind of one of God's children, sad indeed will be your end. Divine justice will sooner or later deal

with you as you deal with others. Let your life at all times be marked by simplicity of character, and pure and holy acts. Learn to love your neighbor as yourself; but love the personality of no man. If you love the personality of another, you draw to yourself, through sympathy, the evils that rule and bind that one to earth.

Our Lord and Master, Jesus, said, "If any man come to me, and hate not his father, and mother, and wife, and children, and brethren, and sisters, yea, and his own life also, he cannot be my disciple." St. Luke xiv. 26. This is a statement from the highest authority, whose language is unmistakably plain and emphatic. It shows, without a shadow of a doubt, the attitude of mind required by all who would obtain discipleship of Christ. The word "hate," used in this connection, means to repel, and is not to be accepted in the sense of desiring that evil befall those with whom we associate. God never commands his children to direct an evil wish or an evil thought toward a fellow-man, but he does command all who would attain to "his likeness" to repel those things which in any way hinder the unfoldment of a spiritual consciousness. If we do not repel the evils active in those we have loved, we will remain one with the great body of humanity, we will never be able to withdraw from it, which we must do if we would obtain righteousness and freedom from the flesh.

Each one who travels the way of righteousness must indeed realize that "he is despised and rejected of men; a man of sorrows, and acquainted with grief" (Isa. LIII. 3), for this road is so narrow that but one can go that way at a time. He who endeavors to take another with him, entails upon himself insurmountable difficulties; sooner or later he will realize that his responsibilities are greater than he can possibly bear, and he will be forced to relinquish his burden and proceed alone. Far better is it to leave the burden behind in the beginning, than to carry it for a time, and then find that he has undertaken more than he can hope to accomplish. This life—while in the beginning very

difficult and full of sorrow, by reason of breaking away from
the old ties and associations—is, nevertheless, productive of
many sacred and holy joys and pleasures, unknown to the lustful sons of men. As you begin to recognize a spirit consciousness, you will realize that the angel world is drawing closer
and closer to you; and if you persist, and desire knowledge for
the sole purpose of assisting humanity, an angel will walk beside you to guide and instruct, to shed the light of his presence
around you, and to illuminate your pathway. If you labor un-
selfishly you cannot go astray. Isaiah the prophet of God tells
us, "Yahveh shall guide thee continually, and satisfy thy soul
in drought, and make fat thy bones: and thou shalt be like a
watered garden, and like a spring of water, whose waters fail
not." Isaiah LVIII. 11. The angel that Yahveh sends to you,
will point out the pitfalls in your path and all the dangers that
menace you. However, do not endeavor to lean for support
upon, or expect strength from, this heavenly guide; you must
learn to stand alone, learn to depend upon the power of God
to strengthen and support. When you have done the best you
possibly can, then look for help—not before. The presence of
the guiding spirit is very real to some; to others the guidance
comes as the "silent voice speaking within;" to yet others it is
revealed through the illumination of the mind, each one receiving according to his needs and in the way necessary to his peculiar requirements.

The guidance of the Spirit will continue with, and will reveal itself according to the need of the student, until he passes
through the first three Degrees (of which there are seven) of
his attainment, and has entered well into the Fourth. After
the student has passed into the Fourth Degree, the guidance
gradually withdraws, leaving him apparently alone, with no
light from the Spirit. The first three Degrees mark the childhood of the student; they are Degrees of preparation. When
he enters the Fourth he is nearing manhood, and must hence-
forth pass onward alone, depending for guidance upon the

spiritual consciousness that he has developed, and living by the light of the knowledge gained in the previous Degrees. In this Degree his strength and fortitude are tested to the utmost, in order that his abilities and powers may be proven. If he is found worthy, and his dedication to God has been complete as far as he is able to comprehend it, preparation is made to admit him into the Royal Fifth. The Fifth Degree is the entrance, as it were, to the world of cause. It is the Degree of the Nazarite, or rather the entrance to that sublime degree,— the Sixth. The promise made by the angel to the neophyte of the Sixth Degree is this: "Him that overcometh will I make a pillar in the temple of my God, and he shall go no more out: and I will write upon him the name of my God, and the name of the city of my God, which is new Jerusalem, which cometh down out of heaven from my God: and I will write upon him my new name." Rev. III. 12. To be a Nazarite the student must be entirely separate from the world, and sanctified or made holy by the Spirit; and this condition cannot possibly obtain until the Celestial Sixth has been reached, as no man can dedicate himself, body, soul, and spirit, to God until he has been completely separated from all the ties of earth, until he has become an immortal. In the Fifth Degree man becomes clothed with the spotless garments of everlasting youth. When he enters this Degree he is admitted to the spiritual temple, he meets the holy ones face to face, and becomes a co-worker with them. He now understands that his elder brother Jesus Christ did not come to earth to save the souls of men; but to point out the way whereby the physical body could be freed from the taint of sin, which is death, and made immortal, through becoming subservient to the spirit within. This knowledge led the apostle to exclaim, "Death is swallowed up in victory."

The entrance to the Temple of Wisdom is at the end of a dark and fearful passage leading from the Fourth Degree. When the student reaches this dark passage, he is prepared for death. If he enters, he can never return, never again labor with the sons of earth, as one with them; he is dead to the world—as literally as if he were laid in the grave, and the only hope remaining for him is to press onward until he reaches the far end and enters the Temple, never again to return to his labors as a mortal, but as an immortal—or, at least, the possibilities of immortality are within his grasp. Should he, for any cause whatsoever, fail to pass the ordeal which he meets in the dark and narrow corridor, he will be deprived of his physical body, and be forced to enter the realm of souls, there to remain until another opportunity presents itself to him. The dangers and trials to be met in the Fourth Degree are of such a character that no one could possibly describe them; 'it is only necessary to say, that all will be tried wherein they are weakest. Therefore be admonished, and by a life of true self-sacrifice and pure and holy desires, strengthen every link of your armor. Above all, do not allow the yearning of the love nature to mislead you into forming an alliance with the opposite sex. Many men, personally known to the writer, have become hopelessly lost through the lack of power to control their love nature.

In the dark passage man enters the Hall of Judgment where the good and evil deeds of the past are summed up and brought before him, to be judged by him. At some period of his soul's unfoldment the student will realize that God judges no man, but that every man is a judge unto himself. If the good and evil deeds balance, if the ego has become submissive to the higher attributes of spirit, if the heart has become pure and free from unholy desires, if the soul has been purified by having passed through the fires, and if the entire nature has become attuned to the vibrations of spirit, the sins are all wiped out,—man passes onward, a new and higher spiritual being. Should egotism blind the eyes of the soul, or love of praise or fear of blame be still active in the breast, man will find himself in absolute darkness, and if he does not repent, death comes to him in an unexpected way. If all love of earth, all desires for pleas-

ure are eradicated, the student truly dies to all material conditions, and receives the baptism of the Spirit which gives him
immortality, age-lasting life.   When the fullness of the Fifth
Degree has been reached, man will find himself in the realm of
causation and able to command the conditions necessary to his
welfare.

In the Fifth Degree the power of the silent will, the will of
stillness, begins to be manifest.   Previous to this time the neophyte has been the warrior, the positive overcomer of material
conditions.   He has been moving steadily forward conquering,
little by little, the evils, inherited and acquired, which belong
to the lower nature.   He has been building conditions in his
physical body, whereby the divine son, the higher self, can
show forth the wisdom and glory of the Father.   To accomplish all this he has been compelled to use the positive, external
will, the will of execution, the will active in the material world.
Now all is changed; having reached the Fifth Degree, he is
fitted to enter and explore the realm of cause.   As he enters
that realm he realizes the necessity of obtaining an understanding of the laws therein active, in order that he may possess the
necessary powers to labor in that world.   It is the world of
creation into which he has entered, and the will by which he
must rule, is the silent will of stillness, that will which causes
all things to obey, that will which will allow nothing to inter-
fere with the purpose of the Creator.   In this degree the neophyte feels the need of wisdom and discrimination; and in order
to gain wisdom he must draw into his organism, by persistent
silent musing, the principle of love which finds expression in
the nature of the divine Mother.   He must strive to come to
an understanding of that love; he must endeavor to realize the
difference between that love, which is life, and the carnal desire active in the world, which has been mis-called by that
holy and sacred term.   He should bear in mind, that the divine feminine is love, the divine masculine is knowledge; the
child born from the union of these two principles is wisdom.

When man has sufficiently developed the spiritual powers, he enters the Sixth Degree, the Degree wherein the "likeness of the Father" manifests itself. This Degree is the crowning ultimate of the present time; it is here that the flaming sword is lifted; man passes behind the veil, and receives from the formless one, the keys which unlock for him the mysteries of life and death.* It would profit little to dwell upon the grandeur of the perfected souls who have attained to that high and holy degree. Long before man reaches this state, he will have developed wisdom and understanding; he will no longer be dependent upon others for instruction; he will have returned to Eden where he can at all times "behold the face of the Father," having become one with him. Such grand souls are immortal in the broadest meaning of the term; they have overcome death, therefore the grave has no terrors for them.

CHAPTER V.

When God determined to free Israel from the bonds of slavery he selected Moses, a man learned in the knowledge of the Egyptian priesthood, as their deliverer. In order to demonstrate to Pharaoh that God had indeed ordained Israel as his chosen people, it was necessary that Moses should possess greater wisdom and be able to perform greater wonders than the priests and wise men who had been his instructors in the mysteries of magic. That Moses might receive the instruction requisite to fit him for his mission, God led him to the mountain of Horeb (the mount of solitude), where, in a burning bush (God is a consuming fire), he revealed to his chosen servant the great and holy Name.

God's Name, as revealed to Moses, was the sacred Hebrew word of four letters, YHVH, pronounced Yahveh, the literal translation of which is "I will be what I will to be." Ex. III. 14. This holy Name, composed of the four Hebrew letters, Yod, He, Vau, He. is twofold in character; it represents the Theos, or male principle of Divinity, and the Sophia, Wisdom, the divine female principle, the universal Mother-Nature. The first letter, Yod (hand), signifies "the active principle, or power of creation, the supreme will of execution." The second letter, He (window), indicates "the gate to Eden," or the entrance into the heavenly kingdom of the immortals. The third letter, Vau, means "a nail," and symbolizes that all who have incorporated the qualities of the Name into their organism, are allied to the God of the universe, through being able to work in harmony with his will, and are therefore forever "firmly united to the Supreme Mind." The fourth letter, He (window), is a repetition of the second, and represents, or symbolizes, "the second veil, or entrance to the Holy of holies." All who obtain a correct understanding of this Name, by accepting Yahveh as their strength, will realize that they have "power with God and man, and have become masters." To gain this realization they must be obedient to the promptings of the Spirit; otherwise they will call down the fires of infinite wrath, which will consume them. Therefore when you pray that the divine fires may enter, be careful that your thoughts are pure and unselfish, and free from sense desires of any kind.

The Name Yahveh remained with Israel until they defiled themselves by lustful and idolatrous worship. They were repeatedly warned, and admonished to turn from their sinful ways, but they turned deaf ears and sank deeper into sensualism and adultery. Therefore God took from Israel the knowledge of his Name, and, losing it, they lost power and prestige, and eventually were scattered as a nation, and lost to the history of the world. "Behold, I have sworn by my great Name, saith Yahveh, that my Name shall no more be named in the mouth of any man of Judah, in all the land of Egypt." Jer. XLIV. 26. Strange to say, even the learned Hebrews of the present day have not the correct understanding of the great Name of God; but to lost Israel, the seed of Abraham, God's anointed people, the great Name has been revealed anew, and many are beginning to realize that in it lies the secret of true spiritual power, and eternal, conscious life. By God's anointed people we mean, the Christian nations of the earth, who undoubtedly are the lost ten tribes of Israel.

The ancient students of magic understood that in the Name Yahveh was great potency, but they certainly did not comprehend its full importance or the power to be derived from its use: under such conditions they would have realized that "the secret (power) of Yahveh is with them that fear (consecrate themselves to) him; and he will show them his covenant." Psalm XXV. 14. (Read Exodus XIX. if you would become familiar with the covenant promise of God.) Had the ancients been spiritually illuminated, they would have understood the necessity of a life of renunciation and regeneration; God would have revealed his Name to them in all its fullness, and through it they would have gained, what they sought so earnestly, the Elixir of Eternal Youth.

"The Name of the Deity, which we call Jehovah, is in Hebrew a Name of four letters, JHVH; and the true pronunciation of it is known to very few. The true pronunciation is a most secret arcanum, and is a secret of secrets. 'He who can rightly pronounce it, causes heaven and earth to tremble, for it is the Name which rusheth through the universe.' Therefore when a devout Jew comes upon it in reading the Scriptures, he either does not attempt to pronounce it, but instead makes a short pause, or else he substitutes for it the name *Adonai*, ADNI, Lord."—*The Kabalah Unveiled.*

Of the various appellations by which they designated Deity, the Pythagoreans preferred the name Yahveh. They had many others, but this word of four letters they held most sacred. It was considered by them too sacred and holy to be pronounced or familiarly used, therefore they designated God, when used in the sense of the "I will be what I will to be," as "Tetragrammaton." We must here remind the student that the Name Yahveh is a most sacred and holy Name, and must be used only when holy and unselfish ultimates are desired. It should be born in mind that "the value of things is in their use;" therefore, if you value the power of the Spirit, use this word wisely.

In order to arrive at a true conception of the nature of God and the purpose of man's creation and ultimate destiny, the student should remember that God is formless. If you picture God as having form, you clothe him in garments created in your imagination; this makes you an idolator, a worshiper of images. In doing this you break the covenant you have made with the Creator, and cease to have complete trust in his guiding power. God is the mind that fills space: the mind that controls absolutely, and is obeyed without thought of contradiction. He is the life that animates and gives consciousness to all creation. In him is all power, all wisdom, all love. He is the absolute all. If it were possible for man to separate himself for a single moment from God, consciousness would cease, man would be as if he never had existed. The universe sprang into existence at his word, and, by the power of his will, he holds all things in form.

The student who is striving after immortality, must incorporate into his organism those divine powers that will give him dominion over all things. Yahveh, the "I will be what I will to be", represents those qualities; therefore, when man is able to understandingly use the powers represented by that Name, he has at his command unlimited capacity to be what he wills to be. Through this power man has access to wisdom, knowledge, and understanding. As he grows in knowledge and power, he gradually draws himself out from the body of humanity, and forces his way deeper and deeper into those fountains of everlasting youth, flowing unceasingly from the Source of all life. As he separates himself from the material condition of physical life, he begins to realize that he is gradually gaining dominion over the forces ruling that realm. The power governing creation, or generation, is the word of power willed by God into the thought that brought our earth into being. This power governs all planetary life. The command, "Increase and multiply, and replenish the earth," was intrusted to the god of generation, the Elohim. Faithfully are those commands executed; all nature obeys them without question. Man comes under the dominion of this power, the soul of the planet, and were he to remain dependent upon his own strength he would never rise above generation, never enter the eternal sabbath, never become immortal.

As man is carried upward by the currents of evolution, the soul begins to perceive its ultimate destiny. As it begins to understand the purpose of its creation, it looks about for the methods by which it may obtain the necessary powers to enable

it to consummate the will of the Father. When man truly
desires, he establishes the conditions of possession; the soul
prayer ascends to the throne of the Father, and then comes
back the answer, "Therefore I say unto you, What things so-
ever ye desire, when ye pray, believe that ye receive them, and
ye shall have them." St. Mark XI. 24. In order to believe in
and trust God, man must make a covenant of obedience to him;
and before this covenant of obedience can either be made or
ratified, man must understand the meaning of the Father's
Name—not alone intellectually, but also in the soul.

When God created Adam, he created him in his own image, and endowed him with the power to develop his—the
Father's—likeness. Adam was created an immortal spirit,
and for the purpose of giving him the opportunity to grow into the likeness of God he was placed in a beautiful physical
body. He remained pure and holy, without shame, until the
god of generation, the Elohim, forced the desire upon him to
defile his virgin helpmeet Eve. This unlawful act caused Adam
to recognize his nakedness; sin made him ashamed, and he endeavored to hide from God, who, up to this time, "talked with
him face to face." Cain, the first fruit of disobedience, was a
murderer. He was far from being the equal of his father, who
had been created by God, and his birth marked the beginning
of the descent of spiritual man into matter. Adam was an
immortal, and would have remained so had he obeyed the voice
of God. Cain and his progeny were mortals, because they were
born of flesh; they were the offspring of sin, and the result of
sin is death. For ages the race has been descending deeper
and deeper into matter. In our age the descendants of Adam
have become so merged in matter, so under control of the physical senses, that the spirit within is unable to express its true
nature. They have wandered so far from the true path that
they are utterly unable to comprehend spirit. They have gone
as deep into matter as it is possible for them to do; the requisite knowledge has been gained, and the only true course of

life now lies before them. They must either ally themselves to
the Spirit, and rise to a condition of celestial power, or once
more descend, until another cycle passes and another opportunity presents itself. There is only one road to heaven, and
that is found by living the regenerate life. The Kabalists were
very wise when they taught that Yahveh has ordained that cir-
cumcision (symbolizing regeneration) is the way to heaven,
the way to eternal life.

The age in which we live marks the epoch of man's emancipation. Proof of this lies in the fact that the sacred Name of
God is being revealed to the world, and also that great num-
bers are at the present time seeking immortality. "They shall
call on my Name, and I will hear them: I will say, it is my people: and they shall say, Yahveh is my God." Zech. XIII. 9.
The desire for immortality has become almost universal, and we
believe that this desire has caused God again to reveal his Name
to man. "For this cause have I raised thee up, for to show in
thee my power: and that my Name may be declared throughout
all the earth." Ex. IX. 16.

To use the sacred and holy Name of God for selfish or unlawful purposes is a very serious matter, and will entail much
suffering upon all who so use it. Before the student decides
upon the use of the Name, he should be certain that he has
the consent of the soul. Before the consent of the soul can be
obtained the life must be consecrated to God. It is a most
difficult thing to do this,—to renounce the world, and unreservedly consecrate the life to God; yet, unless the consecration
is complete, the promised results cannot be obtained. Unless
the whole nature consents, there will always be a reservation;
and the lower nature will never consent until compelled to do
so by the interior man. Remember that heretofore "many
principalities and powers have ruled your life;" but, if you
dedicate your life to God, you can have no other power beside
him. "He giveth power and strength to his people." Psalm
LXVIII. 35. "I am Yahveh; that is my Name: and my glory

will I not give to another, neither my Name to graven images."
Isaiah XLII. 8.

If the student who makes use of these instructions has not
already consecrated his life to God and renounced all earthly
ties, it is to be hoped that he will pause here, and not attempt
to proceed further until he has done so. The purpose of these
instructions is to show the student how he can draw down the
divine fire. If his thoughts are pure and holy, these fires will
consume all the impurities in the nature, leaving only the
pure refined gold of spirit life; but if the desires are unholy,
they will set on fire all the smouldering, therefore unconquered,
appetites and passions. Unholy desires will cause him to commit errors and indiscretions that will entail untold sorrow and
remorse, and perhaps cause death to the physical organism. "And
Nadab and Abihu, the sons of Aaron, took either of them his
censer, and put fire therein, and offered strange fire before
Yahveh, which he commanded them not. And there went out
fire from Yahveh, and devoured them, and they died before
Yahveh." Lev. x. 1, 2. Be warned by the fate which over-
took these priests in ancient times, and do not attempt to offer
strange fire upon the altar of God. The altar of man's temple is the principle of sex, the fountain of life, of creative energy and power.

God, being the mind and life of the universe, contains within
himself all qualities and principles. Before man attempts to
draw these divine qualities into his nature, he must decide what
is necessary to the ultimation of his purpose. The ultimate for
which man is destined, is to be like God—in his likeness created he man. Therefore if man would unfold that likeness he
must be able to say, "I will be what I will to be." To be able
to say "I will," necessitates the ability to will and to do. This
power may be gained if the following suggestions are faithfully
followed:—

Set apart one hour each day for this purpose, the hour of
sunrise being the best. Use a room occupied only by yourself,

and dedicate it to the service of God. Consecrate all you are
or hope to be to the Holy Spirit, the unformed ocean of deific
mind that fills all space and controls all life; and fervently
desire that that mind will accept the dedication, and take full
possession of your room. When you have dedicated your room
to God, look upon it as a most sacred place, a temple in which
you are to worship him.   Before you enter this room,—if you
wish for certain results—be absolutely sure that your mind is,
free from hatred, anger, jealousy, passion, or any evil thought
or desire. Try to feel in a holy frame of mind, at peace with
your own soul and with all mankind. Strive to realize the sa-
credness of the presence you are endeavoring to draw to you,
and the high ultimate you have in view. Have as little furni-
ture in your room as possible, and let that be of such a character that you can frequently wipe it with a damp cloth.   Avoid
having carpets on the floor, or paper on the walls; these hold
the old magnetic conditions which you throw off, and which are
detrimental to your purpose. If you faithfully carry out the
above instructions, you will be conscious that, when you enter
your room after a day of worry and struggle, the Spirit is there
to receive you, and that the Father's love is also there, to renew
and strengthen your determination.

Have a seat (a strong wooden chair is best for your purpose)
especially for your own use, and permit no one else to sit upon
it. We also advise you to allow no one to enter your room except those who are in full sympathy with your purpose, and
who realize that your room is your temple, your holy sanctuary.
Take your seat facing the east, body erect but not tense: have
your lower limbs from the hips to the knees horizontal, from
the knees to the feet perpendicular to the body; hands resting
lightly on the knees.. See to it that the head, neck and chest
are always in a perpendicular line. You cannot think spiritual
thoughts if the chest is in a cramped position; nor should you
permit the head to droop and rest upon the chest, as this posture
is very injurious, both mentally and physically. Be sure that

your chair is the right height to permit of this. Sitting in this
position permits the magnetic and electric currents to pass
through you without friction. Having seated yourself in the
proper position, "be still and know God." Try to go out into
space, in your imagination, and find the light of Spirit. Try,
with the eyes of the mind, to see a white light, which actually
exists and fills space. This light is God, and when you are
able to perceive it, endeavor to draw it into your organism by
means of the breath, as follows:—

Breathe deeply and fully, as deeply as possible, and from
within repeat the first syllable of the sacred Name,—"Yah." Endeavor to feel the qualities of that Name entering your being,—
qualities which are power to execute the purpose of your will.
If you watch closely you will notice that the breath appears to
start a current at the lower extremity of the spinal column.
This interior current changes the flow of the finer life elements:
heretofore they have flowed downward and outward; now you
begin to turn them upward and inward toward Spirit, and away
from material conditions. This current is the means by which
the magnetic elements—which by the power of transmutation
have been separated from the life generated in the sex organ—
are carried to the brain, the instrument through which the
mind acts, a process which results in the vivification and illumination of that organ. The elements carried to the brain are
those desired by the interior mind, and as the interior mind is
seeking "likeness of God," the qualities represented by the "I
will be" are drawn upward.

As you exhale the breath, interiorly repeat the second syllable of the sacred Name,—"Veh." This part of the drill, as the
student will readily perceive, starts a downward current, which,
when joined to the one flowing upward, creates a wheel that, once
started, continues to run of its own volition. After you remain
in this position for a while, your body will become rigid. This
is as it should be, as it makes you positive to, and proof against,
external influences of an evil character. Keep the interior

nature negative, or open to the inflow of divine power, and be sure you do not lose consciousness, or become entranced. If you do so, you will run great danger of being controlled; and instead of developing into a son of God, you will find that you have become a medium through which unclean spirits seek to manifest their depraved instincts.

After you have started the currents and found the Spirit Light, endeavor to abstract the consciousness from the brain by running the thought, "I am spirit," up and down the limbs. Do not neglect to keep inspiring the Name, "Yah — Veh." You must keep the currents active while engaged in sitting. If you find that you can abstract the consciousness from the brain, endeavor to centralize it in the sensorium of the heart, the organ of sensation and emotion. Be careful, however, not to continue the concentration there—especially if you belong to an interior sign or to the head of a trinity—but pass immediately to the feet. Endeavor to feel that you are inside of them, and in imagination try to picture them as luminous with the white light of Spirit; all the old masters taught that man should develop from the feet up. If you find that the feet are not luminous, but dark and cold, persist in your endeavor to make them luminous and filled with life. When all impurities are removed, the illuminating power of the Spirit will cause them to shine. They must be cleansed, as they represent the understanding. If they should burn as with fire, the life that is being transmuted is not properly distributed. To correct this, draw the life from the feet by the power of thought, and diffuse it throughout the body. When you find that the feet are luminous, then with the consciousness draw the light upward to the calves of the legs. As those organs become purified pass on to the next, until you reach the reins,—the small of the back, the region of the kidneys. Dwell in this organ a long while; it is the storehouse for the life, and until it has been purified by the divine light, it will be found to be full of serpents, which, if you are clairvoyant, you can see.

Spend some time in the spinal column. This part of the structure must be absolutely free from all impurities, or the mind
will not be illuminated with the white light; and in that case
the thoughts will be distorted and out of harmony with the
purpose of God. This is so because the finer and more spiritual elements of life pass through the spinal column, from the
reins to the brain. Dwell long in the organ at the base of the
brain; it must be absolutely free from all impurities. This is
the organ that controls animal sensation; and if it is not luminous with the spiritual light, the desires of the lower nature
will be for animal pleasures. When you pass to the front brain,
realize that you are now in those organs that express the higher
mental attributes. The window through which the soul looks
out upon the cause world is situated in the organ of perception,
just above the eyes; the organ of soul-perception being in the
center. When you can illuminate the body from the crown of
the head to the soles of the feet, you are in a position to defy
disease and the unseen powers of the astral world. Do not let
failure deter you from your purpose; make up your mind to
work for years, if necessary, until the desired ends are reached.
But if you persist, and are faithful to your dedication, you will
sooner or later realize that you are not working alone, but that
you are allied to the highest and noblest souls now on earth. You
will also be made to know that these methods have opened for
you the door to the grandest mystic order in existence, whose
temple, though hidden from the eyes of men, does exist. Not
only does this temple exist, but, as they are ready, all will be
led to it, and will be initiated into the sacred mysteries of life,
which cannot be revealed to those who would unwisely use them.

We have endeavored to make these drills as simple as possible. We have not gone as deeply into them, or explained them
as fully, as we would have liked, but we have revealed as much
as has been permitted. What has been given will be sufficient
for the faithful ones; for when higher and holier are needed,
One will be present to make the necessary suggestions. As

you tread the road in sorrow and in tears, be cheered, dear faithful souls, with this thought: You are left alone only because it is the wisest plan for you. Your brothers, bound to you by ties stronger than the ties of earth, continually watch and give aid when it is needed. They are invisible to you now, but there will assuredly come a time when the veil will be rent asunder, and you will stand face to face, not only with Him who has you directly under his charge, but with all the Brotherhood,—those who still labor on the visible plane, and those who have passed on to the higher uses in the invisible section. May the peace and love of God abide with you until that time arrives; and may you be able to drink from the "fountain of living waters," which give eternal life.

CHAPTER VI.

CONSCIOUS SLEEP.

The student who is striving to obtain eternal consciousness should bear in mind the fact that, if he is unable to retain consciousness during sleep, he is still under the law of death, still far from the goal of his desires. The heavy, unconscious stupor, so common to all men, and which is considered the correct method of obtaining rest, is wholly a condition of the animal world, and does not by any means rejuvenate the body; on the contrary, persons who indulge in the unconscious sleep, frequently awake feeling dull, heavy, and unrested. To sleep unconsciously is to permit elementary forces free access, and the consequence is that they rob you of the finer magnetic elements so essential to perfect health and vigor. If the body is unprotected during sleep, the old fetid magnetic emanations of your associates, are drawn into it, causing you to feel dull and stupid when you awake.

The immortal spiritual man never for a moment lets go the power of forming intelligent thought. It is true that as long as he retains the physical body he will permit it to sleep: sleep with him, however, is not a state of stupor, but a time for recuperating the body. During the period of sleep the soul is free from the body, and enters the higher realm of mind, or rather the realm of mind to which his desires ally it, where it lives and labors in a conscious condition. The condition of the consciousness of the soul must ever remain a mystery to unregenerated man. Too much sleep is harmful to any one; four or five hours of such rest should be sufficient for the man who is conserving all the energies—of course, those who are squandering the precious life require more. As the question of sleep is very important, we offer the following suggestions to the student.

Before retiring devote a few minutes to silent meditation, in order that the mind may be quieted and made receptive, in preparation for the labors which you, the spiritual man, intend it shall perform.   Bear in mind the thought, that the subjective mind, the soul, controls the physical body, its sensations, appetites, and passions; but it will obey the promptings of the objective mind, the intellect.   This being true, auto-suggestions are not only valuable but necessary to the man who is striving to overcome the evils.   The suggestions, however, must be clearly defined and impressed upon the soul without a mental reservation. If there are reservations, the mind cannot impress the thought with sufficient power of will to accomplish the results desired; at least the results will be effected only in a degree corresponding to the amount of force and fixedness of purpose possessed by the objective mind.

Upon retiring suggest to the subjective mind the necessity of watching the body and guarding it from those enemies who, unless the soul is on guard, will assuredly rob you of the precious gold which you are endeavoring to store up.   But at the same time remember that the thought must not be impressed upon the soul that you doubt its ability to care for the body; such a thought will be sufficient to cause the subjective consciousness to disregard the promptings of the intellect.   You must also impress upon the subjective consciousness the necessity of a perfect physical body.   These suggestions the soul will obey. Of course you must not expect the body to change immediately; were it perfectly plastic it would do so, but as it is not, some time must elapse before the auto-suggestions are manifest to the external senses. If you find that they are not manifested, you may rest assured that there is a reservation, or a doubt, still existing in the objective mind, which prevents it from expressing the thought with sufficient power to insure obedience.

The student who is striving to gain control of the god of sleep—one of the most subtle enemies he meets—should, upon

retiring, hold the mind in the same attitude of watchfulness as
a man would naturally hold were he compelled to sleep among
thieves with a great treasure in his possession. If he can avoid
it, he should never sleep upon a feather bed: a hard hair mat-
tress is much to be preferred. The bedclothing should be as
light as possible. Do not, however, go to extremes here, and
try to do with less than the needs demand; you should sleep
warmly, but at the same time avoid having too much weight on
the body. Have your room well ventilated, and when possible
sleep with the windows open. Have your windows so arranged
that they can be pulled down from the top as well as raised
from the bottom, and be sure to avoid draughts. If it can be
so arranged, never sleep in your living room. If you have two
rooms, do not sleep with a fire in your bed chamber, and never
permit strangers and inharmonious persons to enter it; it should
be sacred to the purpose to which you have dedicated your life.
Have your sittings in your bedroom, as long as the weather
permits: of course, in cold weather use your living room, unless
you can warm your bedroom sufficiently by leaving the door open
between the two apartments. Never sleep in the same garments
that you have worn during the day; and if you take the daily
baths, as you should, do not change your nightrobe oftener
than once in two weeks. If you are living a pure and holy
life, and are conserving the vital fluids, the magnetic elements
retained by the nightrobe, which should be of soft material,
will be beneficial to you. Never sleep in a room into which the
sun does not shine, and at least once a month allow the rays of
the sun to touch every part of the body. Until you have gained
control of the sex function do not take a sun bath oftener than
once a month; the sun is a generator of life, and until you have
control, you already have all the life you can utilize. Never
sleep with a high pillow under your head; if you must use one,
let it be hard and low. It would be better to do altogether
without pillows, especially in the case of persons who have been
breathing through the mouth, and who are endeavoring to
breathe, as they should, through the nose.

Each one being differently constituted, no absolute rule can be given as to the position in which to lie. The writer gives the methods he has found suited to his own requirements:— Lie flat upon your back, with the head toward the north, hands placed upon the sensorium of the heart, left hand covering the right; cross one foot over the other, the left foot uppermost. At first this position will be difficult to maintain, but after you have become accustomed to it, you will find that you better retain the magnetic and electric elements within yourself; and as you must conquer old habits, this manner of sleeping may prove a help in that direction. Sleeping in this position helps to close the door to adverse currents and psychisms. After you have gained soul consciousness, and can control the life, you will find it much better not to cross the limbs, but to admit the free entrance of the magnetic and electric currents; you will also be able to determine the position best adapted to your requirements. If you watch closely you will also find that the position in which you rest affects the mental and sleep consciousness to a remarkable degree. As you lie in the different positions carefully study the mental states, and you will soon be able to determine whether you should sleep with your head north, south, east, or west; then sleep in the position you find best suited to your needs. Should you be restless during sleep, change your position until you can determine which position is productive of quiet, and which one produces restlessness; you can frequently obtain the desired quiet by standing with your bare feet on the ground, turning your face toward the east. Choose at all times the quiet; for, remember you are striving to arrive at a state in which all the senses can be stilled.

When you have determined upon the position that you intend to adopt, quietly settle yourself, and try to realize that the body has been laid down to rest, but that the real man, living as he does in an ocean of life, never rests; he labors on, ever on, until he reaches a state of continual rest, which is the rest of service. As you quietly lie upon your bed, hold the mind passive to the will of the Spirit, but positive to all thoughts foreign to your purpose; fix your mind on the Infinite, in loving trust, and desire strength and wakefulness. Breathe through the nose, slowly and regularly. As you breathe in this manner, strive to realize that you have started an interior breath, the soul breath, the breath of life, the feminine breath of God; the breath which Yahveh breathed into Adam, and which made him a conscious, immortal man; a breath which he lost when he fell from a state of regeneration to one of generation. The interior breath vivifies and strengthens the powers of the soul. It is a breath that can be felt by a sensitive person who possesses soul unfoldment: it appears (perhaps not to all alike) as a sensation of quiet rising and falling in the interior,—a sensation which manifests itself in the Virgo function of the body. Try to realize that the external atmosphere which you are breathing contains many elements besides those known to science: it contains the life elements of our Father,— the positive life elements which are being incorporated into your organic structure, enriching your blood and giving power and strength to all your faculties. It is illuminating your brain and quickening the power of the intellect, making you a superior creature in every sense of the word. As your finite mind assimilates the life and mind of the Infinite, you will gradually cease to express the mind of the mundane, and begin to express the mind and will of the celestial world. Try at this time to realize that you are, as it were, at the center of an unlimited ocean of pure, divine life, which knows no disease, pain, sorrow, or death; that it is ever conscious, ever doing, ever forcing all creation onward, with a mind and will that nothing can resist. If you resist that mind and will you begin to struggle and are thrown into confusion; if you work in harmony with it, you will be filled with that nameless peace, that peace which passeth understanding, that peace unknown in any realm of consciousness other than that of spirit.

In order to gain a soul consciousness you must with an un-
wavering determination hold to the foregoing thoughts; when
they have become a part of your being, you will realize that
you have passed from death unto life, that you can readily
comprehend the divine mysteries of Godlikeness, and are able
to unlock the door of the spiritual kingdom.   If you can develop sufficient strength to say, "I will," you can unlock the
door of the soul, can lift the veil, can explore the hidden chambers therein, can turn the eyes within and behold the glories of
our Father's kingdom.   When you can do this, you will be
amazed at the wondrous power and love of God, and a holy
and unspeakable joy will fill your soul with praise to Him in
whose image and likeness you were created; sublime and sacred
truths will be revealed to you, such truths as are withheld from
those who dwell with mortals, and are satisfied with material
dross.

Should the student, after he has retired, find that he is unable to hold a definite line of thought, or to retain an active
interior consciousness, but is sinking into that state of stupor
which is literally death, it may be necessary to resort to drastic
means in order to accomplish the desired object.   We suggest
that he try the following methods:—

Spring from the bed, without allowing the external senses an
opportunity to remonstrate, and proceed at once to sponge your
body all over with cold water, and afterwards rub it with a
coarse towel until it is dry and warm.   When it has been rubbed
dry, clothe yourself in loose garments that will permit the air
to have free access to all parts of the body; walk briskly up and
down the room until your body glows with the energies you
have brought into activity.   When your body and brain have
become active, quietly seat yourself in your chair, in an easy
reclining position.   Now try to realize that you have access to
the fountain of living waters, the divine life, which is filled
with potential energy and vigor.   Try to draw this creative
life into your body, in order to recuperate the energies: at the

same time through auto-suggestion impress the soul, the conscious, thinking, immortal man, that it does not require to sleep, that it must not sink into a state of unconsciousness, but must ever remain on guard to protect its servant, the physical body. The interior man is spirit, therefore he must always remain consciously engaged in forming thought. Remember that you are striving to grow into the likeness of Him who never slumbers nor sleeps. You must ever remain conscious, ever press onward toward the goal you have set before you, ever realize that you are equal and one with the angelic hosts, who press around the Father's throne, and continually cry, "Hosanna to the Lord on high." When the body feels tired, again retire. If, as before, you feel that you are falling into an unconscious condition of mind, arise and repeat the drill. Do this time and again, even if you have to pass the night without sleep; but do not attempt this severe method until you have made some progress in retaining the seed. We also advise women not to attempt to follow these directions; they are differently constituted and cast in a finer and more delicate mould than is man. The arch-natural woman stands in the life centers; the arch-natural man is the expressor of the mind of God.

No régime can be intelligently laid down by which woman can obtain conscious sleep. A positive woman may with safety follow the suggestions given to men; a negative woman cannot. She should use great discretion and discrimination in the matter of obtaining rest; and endeavor by every method at her command to retain the finer and more vital elements, which are continually flowing out to her associates, even though she be unaware of the fact. She should endeavor to establish a tranquil state of mind, refusing to be worried, or to be led into such scenes of gaiety or excitement as will arouse the imagination, or cause unhappiness or inharmony; both of the conditions last named are productive of a mental state detrimental to the conservation of the life forces. She should so arrange her mode of living that she may be able to take needed rest whenever

she feels the strain of undue fatigue. She must remember,
however, that a heavy, unconscious sleep will not rest her nearly
so well as will the quiet, semi-conscious, interior musing. When
she becomes conscious of receiving new and more spiritual life
potencies, she must be careful not to build ideal states and
associations, but should centralize her thoughts on God our
Father, with a desire that the gathered life may be wholly dedicated to him and to the elevation of humanity. Woman's call-
ing is a high and holy one: the present cycle marks the time
when she is to be emancipated, when she is to be freed from
the bondage of sin, consequent upon the fall. She is now to
occupy her true place by the side of her brother man, as his
equal and divine helpmeet.

The student who is compelled to resort to the foregoing
methods may, and undoubtedly will, find that he is very tired
the next day, feeling almost unable to perform his duties; but
if he keeps the will active, he will be surprised to realize that he
is not as tired as he had expected to be. Repeat the drill, night
after night, until success crowns your efforts. You will fail
many, many times; but gradually a new consciousness will
awaken within, and when it does, you will quickly realize that
the state which you before looked upon as consciousness, was
but a dream from which you have awakened to find yourself in
a condition of spiritual consciousness that is everlasting.

You are striving to become a son of God, therefore need not
lose the consciousness in order to obtain bodily strength and
mental vigor; just the reverse is necessary. When you gain a
soul consciousness that neither slumbers nor ceases from active
labor, you will require very little sleep; and when you do awaken
from your conscious sleep, you will be strengthened and invig-
orated, filled with power and understanding. If you persist in
your endeavors to sleep consciously, in time you will be surprised to realize that your body has fallen asleep, but that you,
the real, conscious, undying man, have all the higher faculties
awake and active. You may now watch and study the sleeping

body; it may rest in perfect security, for the master is awake
and on guard, ever ready to repel the adversary who would attempt to approach and disturb his servant.   You will now
realize that your physical body is but an animal to be used by
you, who are a spiritual son of God.   When you can realize
this, you have made much progress toward your ultimate goal.

One of the greatest barriers to soul growth has been the fact
that man has looked upon the physical body as the real entity,
when it is only a covering, a cloak, that hides the thinking
spirit, the real ego.   It is of earth, earthy, and continually
changes, eventually returning to the elements from which it
was created.   The divine ego, the celestial word, which animates the physical body and gives man the capacity to unfold
his true nature, will ever urge him forward to more exalted
spheres of labor and consciousness.   It was created in the image of God, therefore, like the Father, it cannot die, but ever
draws nearer and nearer to the Source from which it emanated,
until finally the time will arrive when the likeness of the Father
shall have been unfolded.   Then the ego, having balanced all
sides of the nature, will realize its true divine, immortal state.
When the elements and environments with which the soul has
been surrounded, and which have limited its freedom of action,
have been removed, the real man will stand forth in all the
glory of his kingly power, unrestricted in his actions, unlimited in his capacity to do and be what he desires.   Then he
will fully understand the true significance and power of the
Holy Word Yahveh, the "I will be what I will to be."   Then
he will be an accepted son, who, although a dweller among
men, will be perfected in the divine likeness of his Creator.
Then, and not until then, will man fully realize that he has
thrown off the mortal garb of earth and has put on the immortal garment of spirit-consciousness, which gives agelasting life.

The student must not infer from what has been said about
"conscious sleep" that the consciousness referred to is the same
as the mental state which he has regarded as consciousness; it

is far different.   So different is it, and so superior to the state
recognized as consciousness, that it is difficult to describe.
When one awakens to the external consciousness, he is not at
all times able to recall all that he has experienced, but he has
in the interior, a feeling of knowing, such as he has never felt
before.   There are many reasons why the experiences of the
spirit life are not revealed to, or remembered by, the physical
man.   One reason is that those thoughts that we are able to
recall, or image in the brain, have been created from the life
of the body.   The thoughts in the interior mind have been
created from higher qualities of life than the external man can
use or know anything of; and as they have been created outside the sphere of the brain, it is unable to image them, therefore has not the power to call them up, or, as it is termed, "remember" them.

If man persists in his endeavors to gain an unceasing consciousness, there will come a time when the interior spiritual
self will have absolute control over the external consciousness.
When this power has been gained the ego can return into the
objective consciousness very cautiously, and, as it returns, it
can impress upon the brain the image of the thoughts and experiences of the subjective state.   When the ego can do this the
brain will be able to picture these thoughts, and will know in
the external what has taken place while the body has been
sleeping.   As the student develops soul consciousness, he will
realize that there are many things that he does not desire to
bring into the objective mind.   These thoughts are, however,
stored in the soul memory, to be brought into the external when
need for them arises in the life of the individual.   The soul is
wiser than the external man, and will therefore reveal only
those things that are of use.

The dream state lies in the borderland between the lower
and the higher consciousness.   It is a condition or state where
the subjective and objective consciousness overlap.   Dreams
are the reflection, or impressions from the astral realm, which

the external mind receives as it awakens to a consciousness of
earthly surroundings. There are many kinds of dreams—some
are useful, being the thoughts of holy men reflected upon the
mind, to serve as warnings of approaching danger; or they may
be caused by astral conditions and be prophetic of coming
events; they may also be reflections upon the mind by elemen-
tals that would strive to deceive and mislead. No dream can
be relied upon as being useful or as conveying a warning or
as being prophetic, unless it is very vivid, and its meaning
and purpose firmly impressed upon the mind as the individual awakens to the external. The Holy Ones will never reflect thoughts upon the brain, causing a dream, unless they impress the meaning of it upon the mind. Of course the student
must remember that the language of the spirit world and of
God, is a language of form. It therefore follows, that the animals, objects, and things, as well as the conditions experienced
in the dream state, can be interpreted only by those who are
familiar with the language of symbology, or the use and purpose of form. The Bible is a sealed book to all except those
who have been spiritually illuminated, because it was written
by holy men who were familiar with the language of God, and
who wrote as the Spirit dictated, so that only the wise would
understand.

When the student awakens in the morning he should not
permit himself to lie and idly dream. If he does he will assuredly fall asleep, and will often find to his sorrow that the
adversary has robbed him of the precious treasure he has striven
so laboriously to store up. The time of greatest danger is in
the early morning hours, and if the student would only remember that the body of a healthy man will not awaken naturally
until it has had sufficient sleep, he would have fewer regrets,
and would be brighter and more capable of performing his duties. When you awaken you should arise at once. Do not
allow the senses to persuade you from doing this, but instantly
spring with a quick, positive motion upon the floor. Imme-

diately upon arising take a cold-water bath, regardless of the
cold or disinclination to do so. In doing this you will increase
the power of the will and develop the stoic. If you take control of the body with a positive will, the senses will soon become
what God intended them to be; namely, faithful servants, not
masters. When you have taken your bath, rub yourself with
a coarse towel until the circulation is restored and the energies
brought into activity. (Those who have not robust health should
modify the bath to suit their physical condition, but should strive
by all means at their command to make their bodies healthy
and strong.) After rubbing the body perfectly dry, clothe
yourself, and then take exercise of such a nature as will harmonize body and mind; a quick, positive walk, with the consciousness active in the body, will, as a rule, be all the exercise
you will require. When you have finished your walk, return
to your room and turn your attention to the methods already
given for inspiring *the will*. After you have finished your concentration, if it is still too early for you to begin the labors of
the day, turn your attention to the mind, and endeavor to
put into order the thoughts you have been formulating. If
you do this you will find that the thoughts gathered are of such
a nature as will be practical and useful to your further attainment.

Before leaving this subject, we would call our readers' attention to the fact that they should sleep consciously if they
would reach the land of promise. In Holy Writ we read that
before the children of Israel could enter the promised land,
they had to overthrow the kingdom of Bashan, which, translated, means "sleep." So will you have to overcome the king
of Bashan, if you would enter the kingdom which the Lord
our God has prepared for all who will conquer the old Levi-
athan, the monster that has thrown the race into a state of
stupor. Again we read, "The kingdom of heaven suffereth
violence, and the violent take it by force." St. Matt. xi. 12.
Only the violent—the strong of purpose—will ever pass as an

immortal, from earth, the home of mortals, to the celestial land
of promise.   May God give to all seekers after truth, wisdom
and understanding, and powers that will enable them to let
their light so shine that the world will perceive and realize
that righteous sons of God live and move among men; and may
they bring the truth to those still in darkness, thus blessing
the race by their presence, and creating holier and brighter
conditions for the sons of men.   Our prayer is, that the truths
which we have expressed, may awaken in the soul of the devout
Christian higher aspirations, and a broader comprehension of
the fact which Jesus demonstrated:—

Man cannot die!
'Tis true the mortal coil
To dust and ashes doth return
When it has served its use.
The true, the animating spark,
The star divine,
Image of Him who did
The universe create, doth not
Depend on mortal breath,
Nor earthly loves, its span to eternize.
In proud preeminence it roams
From sphere to sphere—
It is not bound; the broad expanse
Of space its course doth trace,
Unmeasured by the highest sense
Of finite mind.

FINIS.

℣ ℣ ℣ THE ESOTERIC ℣ ℣ ℣

A FIFTY-PAGE MONTHLY MAGAZINE.

THE ESOTERIC is devoted to methods, scientifically religious, for bringing body, mind, and soul into harmony with God and nature.

Those seeking Holiness of heart and life should read it.

Also those who are studying magic will find in it the secrets of the Power of the Christ, of his knowledge, and of his understanding.

We accept as a foundation of all, the following: God is the Creator of *all* things; therefore all laws, physical, mental or spiritual, are but the potency of the divine mind. To know that mind (or the laws or methods produced by its action, which is divine) is the highest physical, mental and spiritual attainment of man.

Because of this we study every department of nature, and endeavor to give to the world such facts as we deem most advantageous in the development of our race.

Published by THE ESOTERIC PUBLISHING Co., Applegate, California; formerly of 478 Shawmut Avenue, Boston, Mass.

TERMS.

Per year (for United States and Canada)...$1.00
Per year (foreign).. 1.25
Six months (United States and Canada)... .50
Six months (foreign)... .65
Single copies.. .10

BOUND VOLUMES OF THE ESOTERIC.

Bound volumes of THE ESOTERIC magazine, from its first issue, are obtainable, neatly put up, at the uniform price of $2.00 each, in cloth.

The first four volumes have been revised and consolidated, making but two. Volume I. should be read by all who are seeking unity with God, as it contains a series of «Practical Instructions» for reaching the highest goal of human attainment, which is in itself a complete occult library. The laws explained therein will, if conscientiously followed, lead the student to the highest goal of his desires.

In Volume II. begins a series of «Bible Reviews» and helps by H. E. Butler, which we cannot too strongly recommend. These reviews run through several volumes, and, being associated with other suggestive writings on line of Esoteric development or soul unfoldment, will be found exceedingly helpful and instructive to the student.

PRACTICAL METHODS TO INSURE SUCCESS.

This booklet is a special guide to young men and women who wish to reach the highest ultimates of life in any and all departments, including a pure, Christian life. The rules laid down are so plain and simple that children from ten to eighteen years understand them better than those of mature age, whose lives have been perverted by false habits. Their practical value and reliability have been proven in America and Europe by thousands of young and old of both sexes. Hundreds of the ablest medical practitioners of every school indorse and highly recommend them as being the true and safe road to success. The methods set forth in this booklet will produce surpassing vigor of health and power of mind, and add a magnetism that will enable the possessor to carry all before him. This little book, a pocket edition of 104 pages, is distributed by the Esoteric Publishing Co., on receipt of 10 cents. Bound in cloth, 25 cents.

Address, ESOTERIC PUBLISHING Co., Applegate, California.

THE ZODIACAL INDICATOR.

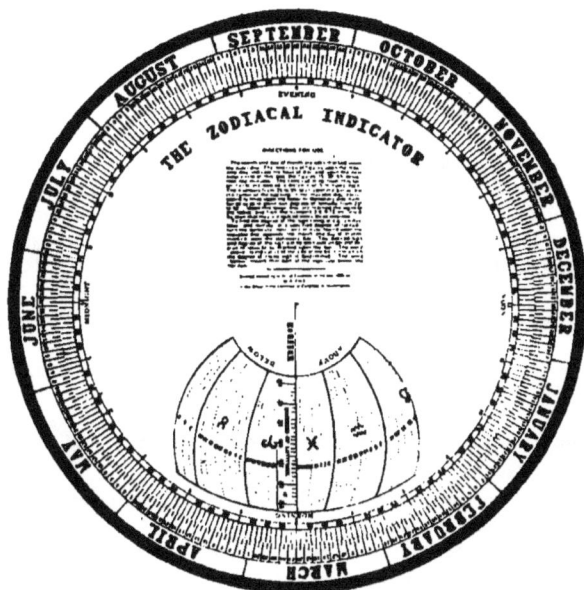

This instrument is probably the most perfect mechanical device yet constructed for finding the rising sign, as it gives the degree and minute of that sign's elevation above the horizon for any Latitude between 22° and 55°, which embraces nearly the whole civilized world. It will be a great convenience to astrologers; and those who doubt the influence of the zodiacal signs, or those who wish to experiment upon such influence, will find,—by having this Indicator at hand and watching the change of their mental and physical states with the changing signs,— that not only will their own experience convince them of the reality of zodiacal influence, but that a new field of experimentation, most interesting and profitable, will open up to them. (Every one is not sufficiently sensitive to feel these changes, but, in most instances, the observer will be quite conscious of them.) The Indicator is neatly and durably constructed, and, with proper care, will last for years. Price $1.00.

REGENERATION: THE GATE OF HEAVEN.

A most complete and satisfactory summary of evidence in favor of the life of regeneration, embodying the results of exhaustive scientific research: Biology, Physiology, the Bible, Philosophy, Sacred and Profane History, Art, and Poetry, also the opinions of leading Scientists, are all brought into requisition and caused to bear testimony to the regeneration. No honest sceptic can read this book without being convinced of the truth, importance, and benefits of the life. Those who stand *alone* in the regeneration should place this book in the hands of those around them. Cloth, post-paid, $1.25.

ESOTERIC PUBLISHING COMPANY, Applegate, California.

☙ESOTERIC EDUCATION☙

Or the Unfoldment and Life of a Hero.

Translated from the German of J. Kernning's «Key to the Realm of Spirit.»

The narrative of knight Geoffrey, subsequent to his esoteric training, contains a report of the young hero's feats, sufficiently detailed to give a clear idea of the way in which spiritual insight and powers work together to make the prepared and purified man an invincible conqueror. Thus this book may encourage mothers of deep thought and faith, like Lady Mathilda, to give their sons also the education of heroes, making them instruments to solve the problems of modern society, as there is no age without its opportunity and need for heroism. Cloth, post-paid, 50 cents.

THE NARROW WAY OF ATTAINMENT.

A SERIES OF SPECIAL INSTRUCTIONS DELIVERED TO THE SOCIETY ESOTERIC.

BY H. E. BUTLER.

With an introductory paper translated from the German by Prof. Wieland.

The thoughts expressed in this book are of such a character as to recommend themselves to all classes. It teaches the old Egyptian method of gaining soul power and leads the student, by plain and simple methods, to where he can understand and utilize the teachings of Jesus, whose life and works demonstrated that he brought to the world the highest cult ever known. Bound in cloth, 140 pages, $1.00, post-paid.

☙WOMAN'S CIRCULAR☙

♥ ♥ ♥ ♥

A booklet of 42 pages, containing special instructions in the Regenerate Life. It has been carefully compiled for those women who are striving to gain true soul powers. The rules laid down are of such a character that all can readily understand them, being clothed in simple language, free from all technical terms and occult phrases. A few months' trial will convince the most skeptical that the methods recommended are not experiments, but are the result of much thought and actual knowledge obtained through personal observation and experience. Price, paper, post-paid, 25 cents.

THE SEVEN CREATIVE PRINCIPLES.

BY H. E. BUTLER.

This book should be read by every student and thinker. It explains the laws of nature in a scientific and lucid manner. It makes clear the process of evolution and development and holds the reader spell-bound with its simple truths.

170 pages. Illustrated. Price, post-paid, $1.50.

Address, ESOTERIC PUBLISHING Co.. Applegate. California.

✿ ✿ ✿ SOLAR BIOLOGY ✿ ✿ ✿

A New Scientific, Exact and Easy Method of Delineating Character; Diagnosing Disease; Determining Mental, Physical
and Business Qualifications, Conjugal Adaptabil-
ity, etc , from Date of Birth.

BY HIRAM E. BUTLER.

Illustrated with Seven Plate Diagrams and Tables of the Moon
and Planets, from 1820 to 1900.

This science proves that «All are members of One Body» (I. Cor. XII. 12–27);
and that, as such, each one has his peculiar function in life. It throws a flood of
new light upon the problems of life, furnishing the groundwork, or scientific law,
which goes down into the *minutiæ* of the life of every man and woman, as a mir-
ror reflecting their innate nature. This work tells what is in man and how derived. Tells how to cultivate self and make the most and best of life. Tells one,
when a child is born, what kind of training it should have, to what diseases it is
liable, how to avoid or how to cure when already developed. Reveals the part of
the grand body to which each individual belongs, and the consequent mental ten-
dencies, physical fitness, natural sphere, and highest and fittest use in the world.

It enables parents to know just what business their children are best adapted
for, and how to educate them, and is also a guide to all persons in the preservation
of health and strength, and an important aid to success and to the attainment of
the great object in life, viz., usefulness and happiness. It also aids in prolonging
the life of old and young. *It is of especial importance to physicians,* enabling
them to attain great success through having in their possession a certain key to
knowledge concerning the nature and peculiarities of their patients such as heretofore has been available only to those few that were possessed of rare intuitive
discernment.

It is claimed that character is expressed in the countenance, that it shapes the
cranium, and is even written in the hand; but Solar Biology introduces the student
into the grand workshop of the Solar System, not only defining character and function, but supplying the key to self-knowledge and harmonious human relatedness;
and, further, it opens up a knowledge and understanding of the principles and laws
by which human evolution is being carried forward, and the infinite variety of
forms and natures brought into being on the planet earth.

SOLAR BIOLOGY makes an elegant octavo volume of 500 pages, heavy paper,
clear type, with author's portrait and appropriate illustrations. Bound in superior cloth, embellished with symbolical designs in gold. *No elaborate study or
preparation is required to enable one to read character and otherwise apply the
science.* The key to the use of the science will be found on page 274, and can be
fully mastered in a few minutes.

PRICE $5.00.

ESOTERIC PUBLISHING COMPANY,

Applegate, Calif.

www.ingramcontent.com/pod-product-compliance
Lightning Source LLC
Chambersburg PA
CBHW020226090426
42735CB00010B/1597